ORGANIZING
you

BUILDING YOUR HOUSE

A Faithful Mom's Guide to
Organizing Home and Family

SHANNON UPTON

Columbus Press
P.O. Box 91028
Columbus, OH 43209
www.ColumbusPressBooks.com

EDITORS
Brad Pauquette & Emily Hitchcock

ARTWORK, DESIGN & PRODUCTION
Columbus Publishing Lab
www.ColumbusPublishingLab.com

Paperback ISBN 978-1-63337-057-9
Ebook ISBN 978-1-63337-058-6

Printed in the United States of America
1 3 5 7 9 10 8 6 4 2

To Travis, who supports my ministry wholeheartedly

To Spencer, Karly, and Oliver, who make me a Jesus Mom

And to Jesus, who walks through my house with me

Building Your House

Contents

My people will live in peaceful dwelling places,
in secure homes,
in undisturbed places of rest.

Isaiah 32:18

Chapter 1

Spiritual Clutter

I organize for Jesus.

I know how that sounds. People's brows furrow when they hear me say that I have an "organizing ministry." How does one do something as secular as organizing and call it a ministry?

Well, I certainly wouldn't have thought of it on my own. My plan was to become a professional organizer, sailing from house to house and helping people clear out their clutter. I was excited to make my own quiet waves for Christ this way, leaving joy, peace, and clutter free spaces in my wake.

But when my youngest child was just one year old, the Lord steered me onto a different course. He took my love of organizing, combined it with my experiences as a wife and mom, added a generous dash of wisdom born from suffering, and wrapped it all up for me in a clear vision: I was to help my sisters in Christ use organization to clear out their spiritual clutter.

He opened my eyes so I could see how all of our spirits are cluttered to different degrees. We all feel anxious, at times, about our lives and how we're choosing to live them. We worry about what we aren't doing that we should be...or what we are doing that we shouldn't.

God gave me a burning heart for women who are struggling with time and household management—which is all of us, at least sometimes! My ministry is based on Proverbs 14, particularly the first verse:

> The wise woman builds her house,
> but with her own hands the foolish one tears hers down.
>
> *Proverbs 14:1*

That's what spiritual clutter really is: the worry that we're tearing down our own houses. It's the sneaking feeling that we aren't being the wives and mothers and daughters of God that we should be. We want so much to be that wise woman, building her house with both hands!

The Proverbs 14 Woman

As I studied Proverbs 14, I found that it offers much more insight into building our homes for our families and our Lord. When we embrace this wisdom, we can become Proverbs 14 Women!

Where there are no oxen, the manger is empty,
but from the strength of an ox comes an abundant harvest.

(verse 4)

It takes work to keep a household running: to keep your house and your kids clean, to keep up with everyone's schedules, and to keep food in the fridge (or in the manger, as it were). You, Jesus Mom, are the strong ox for your family. Through your hard work, there will be an abundant harvest of love, peace, and joy in your home.

The wisdom of the prudent is to give thought to their ways,
but the folly of fools is deception.

(verse 8)

We need to take a deliberate look at the truth. Often, we ignore those thoughts that tell us we need to do things differently, or better. We continue to hoard our spiritual clutter, silencing those little internal warning bells and disregarding our uneasiness. But the folly of fools is deception, and we're no fools. As Proverbs

14 Women, we'll give thought to our ways, facing those anxieties head on and clearing the clutter out of our spirits.

> The house of the wicked will be destroyed,
> but the tent of the upright will flourish.

(verse 11a)

We won't start with the physical clutter—first we need to strive for upright hearts. When we hold our hearts' insecurities up to the light of God's truth, some of them will evaporate. Sometimes we'll have to fight to surrender our worries, pushing them out of our hearts and lifting them up to the Lord. But some of our spiritual discomfort is coming from a place that's pure and true—the Holy Spirit calling us to uprightness. Your spiritual clutter can be the nudge you need to get organized and make a *plan*.

> Do those who plot evil not go astray?
> But those who plan what is good find love and faithfulness.

(verse 22)

You can use organization to clear out your spiritual clutter and make room for love and faithfulness. When you tackle your anxious thoughts, weeding out the lies and bringing the truth to light, the plans that emerge will bring about change to your household! I'm going to help you make these plans as you envision the

home you're preparing to build. You'll be ready for the work—
then you'll have to begin it.

All hard work brings profit,
but mere talk leads only to poverty.

(verse 23)

We can make all of the plans we want, but until we actually
put them into action, there are no rewards. And as Jesus Moms,
we're not doing the work because we want to check off to-do list
items or impress others. We're doing the best we possibly can to
build our homes for the love of our families and the love of our
Lord.

And he who fears the Lord has a secure fortress,
and for his children it will be a refuge.

(verse 26)

When you build your house with both hands, intentionally
for Jesus Christ, you're creating a secure fortress, a refuge for
your family. Your work will affect your whole household—your
husband, your children, the very feel of your home to all who
enter. You'll be creating a peaceful home and allowing the hearts
within to find peace as well.

A heart at peace gives life to the body.

(verse 30a)

A heart at peace gives *life*.

My David Moment

God began to prepare me for this ministry during a period when I was experiencing a complete lack of peace—my heart was bursting with spiritual clutter in a way it never had before.

God introduced me to motherhood with the birth of my son Spencer, and I loved being a mom. Yes, even the first time he threw up all over me, himself, and everything else within a five-foot radius, I loved it. It was three in the morning and I had this sleep-addled thought: *Where is this kid's mom? She's got to come clean this up! Wait, it's me. I'm the mom. I'm the* Mom.

What a joyful realization! Then, when Spencer was almost four years old, my husband Travis and I welcomed our second child. I was blessed to hear the words, "It's a girl." We were elated!

But (you knew there had to be a "but" coming), a few days after Karly was born, I developed a Postpartum Anxiety Disorder. Though I had never heard of PPAD, I learned that many, many women suffer from it. Several of the women I knew opened up and shared their PPAD experiences with me—even though I secretly wished they wouldn't.

I specifically remember a certain mommy acquaintance telling me all about her postpartum time. She told me how afraid she was that she'd drop her baby and the baby would die. I nodded along because I felt exactly the same way. She told me how she was afraid to leave her house or answer the door or phone. This, too, totally rang a bell with me (no pun intended). She told me how she struggled with strange fears, suffered panic attacks, and woke up screaming from nightmares. I was dealing with all of those things on a daily basis.

I knew she was trying to help me feel better by letting me know that I wasn't alone, but all it did was make my burden seem heavier—more real somehow. She was bringing up feelings that I was trying so hard to keep under control. And then came the kicker: she finished her story by saying, "Seriously, those were the worst three weeks of my life."

Three weeks.

Bless her heart, I'm sure those were three terrible weeks for her and her family. But when she told me her story, I was in *year* three. Honestly, I wanted to slug her.

Back around the time my sweet Karly turned a year old, I realized that the various medical professionals in my life had stopped referring to my "PPAD" and had started to refer to my "GAD." I mustered the courage to look it up online and discovered that GAD stands for Generalized Anxiety Disorder. In other words, my postpartum time was over and yet my anxiety was as bad as it had ever been. Meanwhile, I was still waiting desperately for the old me, the *real* me, to return.

When Karly turned eighteen months old, I accepted that this anxious, fearful me *was* the real me now. I spent a few days carrying a very heavy heart, mourning the loss of the life I'd planned. Then one day I woke up with anger burning in my spirit. I knelt by my bed to pray and had what I think of as a David Moment.

Have you ever read a Psalm and thought, *I can't believe David said that to God, the Almighty God! How did he dare?* (You can check out Psalm 58 if you're not sure what I mean.) David could be so blunt, so brazen, so…disrespectful. It seems unbelievable that he talked to God that way—and it's actually recorded in the Bible!

But in our angriest, most frustrated moments, we begin to understand what David surely realized: God knows our hearts anyway, so we might as well lay it all out there and be real. Here's how I started that day:

Lord, I know You promised in Your Word that You're going to bring good out of this, but I can't possibly see how. Maybe You'll bring Travis and me closer together, but right now, even on my best day, I know my anxiety annoys him. Maybe this will draw me closer to the kids...but come on, Lord. I'm down here trying not to scar them for life with my particular brand of crazy. OK, maybe You want me to talk to some anxious woman some day so I can help her...but Lord, I don't think I can help her. None of those anxious "sharers" are helping me!

And then, my David Moment:

Listen, Lord, I DON'T CARE *if You want me to help one woman or five or twenty—it's not enough, God! It's not enough "good" for me to have to suffer this! No one should have to suffer this, Lord! No one should be so constantly afraid of everything all the time. No mom should worry that she'll kill her children by accident. I'll lead some stupid support group if You* MAKE *me, but it won't be enough and I will* NEVER *understand why You're making me go through this.*

I said those things to the Almighty God. If my kids talked to me that way, believe me, discipline would follow. I talked to God that way, yet His love and grace followed. On my knees, I again realized that *I'm the mom*, the mom God chose and equipped to parent my precious children.

After that day, I did my best to live my life for Jesus and my family even with the fear. I began to recognize and address the specific anxieties in my spirit, and I claimed the tools I had to fight them. I learned that a little organization and prayerful planning helped me to relax and feel at peace in my home. I also learned to surrender—my perfectionism, my comparisons to other moms, and my useless, hurtful thoughts.

And then, nearly four years to the day after Karly was born, the Lord blessed me with a healing. On the day my son Oliver was born, the Lord lifted the burden of clinical anxiety from my heart. I need you to understand that this is not typical in any way. All of my doctors said the anxiety would get worse after Oliver was born so I needed to prepare for some really bad times.

But I had prayed that the Lord would use those special nine months to fix whatever had gone wrong in my body the last time, and He did. With praise and thanks and awe, I continued to live my life for Him—but not as the "old me" I had yearned for. Instead, I was a new me who had changed and suffered and grown.

After about a year, wouldn't you know it, God *did* call me to help someone. And not just one anxious woman, or five, or twenty, but many, many women—most of whom had never even heard of postpartum anxiety. They're the women who've heard me speak or have read my first book, *Organizing You: Finding Your Spiritual Clutter and Using Organization to Clear it Out.*

And here's the best part: the day I sent the final manuscript of *Organizing You* to my publisher, I experienced the exact opposite of my David Moment. I sat in front of my computer, ready to hit "send," and was simply overwhelmed. I thought about the two years I'd spent working on the manuscript, hundreds of hours of work. I thought about all of the talks I'd written and practiced and given. And yes, I thought about those four years of clinical anxiety. Then I put my hand on the screen and prayed.

Lord, please bless this work. If just one woman reads this book and grows closer to You, then all of this will be worth it.

How He changes our hearts. For the good, for His Glory. And now I'm praying that God will use my story and my willing heart to bring some of that good to *you*—the mom He chose and equipped to care for your precious family.

Organizing You, The Sequel

Speaking of *Organizing You*, I should mention that *Building Your House* is really a sequel of sorts to my first book. If you haven't read *Organizing You*, you don't have go back and read it (although I'd love it if you did!). You can start right here. Think of it like any great movie sequel: you walk out of the theater having truly enjoyed the movie, but you have a few questions, like who was the guy in black, and why did he have that monkey?

The same concept applies here. As you're reading, you may think, *Is she serious about a paper-based daily planner? What are chore cards and monthly lists? Why is she so obsessed with chocolate? And when am I supposed to find the time to do all this organizing?* The answers to those questions are in *Organizing You*. (Except the chocolate one; there's really no explanation for that.)

Organizing You focuses on the inner woman, on truly organizing *you* as a person. It's a guide to organizing your time, chores, and thoughts. Those things are all foundational to great home organization, and I deeply desire that kind of peace for you. I prayerfully fashioned my first book to help you discover your personal spiritual clutter and create your own personal organizational systems to clear it out.

What you're holding is essentially the second half of that book and an integral part of my ministry message for you—the part about actually running your household. This is the half with the really down-to-earth, actually-get-in-there-and-organize-your-home advice. We're going to use organization to tackle your physical clutter, routines, husbands, and kids—all in the name of Jesus. This is where the rubber meets the road, Jesus Moms!

Just What Is a Jesus Mom, Anyway?

The one thing from *Organizing You* that I really want you to understand is the concept of the "Jesus Mom." Throughout this book I'll be referring to you that way, and believe me, it's a huge compliment. In many ways, the Jesus Mom is the antithesis of the "supermom" our secular world holds up as ideal:

- The Jesus Mom doesn't try to create or present the "perfect" family; she seeks only to please her Lord. (Galatians 1:10)

- Though she plans her days and lives her life she strives to follow God's direction for her life. (٠. 16:3,9)
- She doesn't fuss or mope her way through the tasks in front of her; she does her work for the Lord. (Colossians 3:23)
- She doesn't find her worth (or lack thereof) in her belongings, her appearance, or her homemaking skills; she knows she's worth more than rubies to the Lord who loves her. (I Samuel 16:7, Proverbs 31:30)
- The Jesus Mom wants to live and love and parent and work and run her household with the awareness that Jesus is walking beside her, every moment. (Matthew 28:20)

If you're reading along and thinking, *Yes, Yes, Yes! I want those things, too!* then you're a Jesus Mom already, and this is the organizing book for you.

Building Your House isn't simply about organizing your stuff, it's about building your home on the cornerstone of Jesus Christ and living in His abundance. Your focus on the Lord is what gives your desire to organize your home meaning. The point isn't "having it all" or even having it all together—it's settling our spirits so we can dwell in the Lord's peace.

Peace≠Perfection

Sometimes we think being a Christian means our spirits should be naturally and perfectly clutter free. The Bible says we shouldn't worry about tomorrow, indeed that we shouldn't be anxious in anything. *Hmmm.* If our hearts are for the Lord, then shouldn't peace simply fall on us like a dove?

Sometimes God does bless us with peace that way, but sometimes we have to work for it. At the beginning of my clinical anxiety journey, I felt terribly guilty about my fears, like I was missing an essential element of trust in the Lord that a "true Christian" should have. Then the Lord brought this scripture to my attention:

> Turn from evil and do good;
> seek peace and pursue it.
>
> *Psalm 34:14*

Turn. Do. Seek. Pursue. Those are all things that require action! Over time, I learned to surrender my anxious, harmful thoughts to the Lord. But I also realized that some of my negative thoughts had a basis in truth, in real circumstances that He had equipped me to change.

Jesus Moms, He has equipped us to seek peace and live in His abundance! When you work to clear out your spiritual clutter, you're seeking peace. When you organize your home with Jesus in mind, you're doing good and pursuing peace for you, , - ily members, and everyone in your circle of influence.

As children of God, we want to win people to Him, and clearing out our spiritual clutter can help us do that. God gives us daily opportunities to show His love and demonstrate His peace to our husbands, children, and all we meet. Our ability to respond to these calls could be a potential eternity won...or lost.

If your home is cluttered, you might not invite over your non-Christian friend. If you're hassled at the preschool drop-off because of a stressful morning routine, you could miss the opportunity to help a struggling young mom. If you're holding onto a frustration with your husband, you may complain about him in front of unbelieving coworkers, people who know you're supposed to be a Christian.

If you don't clear out your spiritual clutter, you can hinder your work for the Lord. Jesus Moms, God calls us to more than this. He calls us to turn from evil and do good, to seek peace and pursue it.

One thing He is *not* calling you to is unrealistic perfection. You don't have to have everything "in order" to display a peaceful heart to those around you. Your home doesn't have to look like a magazine cover, your mother's house, or your best friend's. It doesn't matter what you think other people think your house should look like.

I'm not going to tell you what you "should" do to make your home "perfect." You won't be reading about all of the wonderful ways to use over-the-door shoe racks. Instead, I want to encourage you to think about how *you* can build *your* house in a way that will bring peace to your family.

Your goal is whatever makes you feel comfortable and peaceful in your home. Some of you will clear out your spiritual clutter by adding more structure. Some of you will use this process to tweak the good systems you already have. Some of you may find that what you need more than anything is to give yourself some grace. Organization isn't about "all or nothing" perfection, it's a way to settle our hearts so we can live *all in* for God.

Pursuing Peace, For Real

One day when Karly was a few months old, she and Spencer were actually napping at the same time and I found myself with a quiet hour. I decided to mop the kitchen floor with my new and improved mop, the kind with rollers that squeeze the water out of wide sponges. The new mop was bigger than my old one and I discovered I had to push the mop into my little bucket at an angle in order to make it fit.

I swabbed my way across the kitchen and had almost made it to the other side when the mop momentarily stuck in the bucket.

The bucket tipped. By sheer reflex, I quickly righted it, but not before some of the water had sloshed out, hit the wall, and oozed onto the floor.

At this point, you probably would have said, "Drat!" and grabbed a towel, but I was in the grip of an anxiety disorder. I just stood there, frozen with fear and disgust as I watched the puddle of dirty, nasty mop water—on my kitchen floor, in the room where we *eat*—spreading toward my bare feet. The mop water kissed my toes and I lost it. I ran to the farthest corner of the house and had myself a full on panic attack, rocking and crying. It took me the greater part of an hour to get myself together and clean up the mess.

The next time I saw my counselor, I told her what had happened. Now this counselor was what my mom would affectionately call "Hippy Dippy." She didn't style her hair or wear makeup, and she favored clothes like printed t-shirts, broomstick skirts, and sandals with socks. Time didn't seem to matter much to her and she spoke at a plodding pace. Her laid-back ways were starting to frustrate me—I wanted some *results* from my time with her.

So after I told her about the mopping debacle, I asked her, "What should I do when this stuff happens? How can I keep myself from freaking out?"

She steepled her fingers and took a couple of deep breaths. Then she said, very, very slowly, "Shannon…I want you…to get…a bigger…bucket."

Seriously, *a bigger bucket*? How was this helpful? I wasn't talking about mopping, I was talking about dealing with *life*. I told her as much with polite exasperation. This is how she replied:

"Shannon, this *is* how you deal with life. There will always be things that stress you out. You've got to start by recognizing what they are and preventing them. You worry about your kids' safety. Well, stop watching medical dramas and don't watch the news. If you stress out about Spencer climbing on playground equipment, then don't go to the park for a while—he'll be fine. Control what you can first. *Get a bigger bucket*."

She was right. I'd been trying so hard to conquer my anxiety that I hadn't taken the steps to avoid it in the first place. Many of my triggers were right in front of me, just begging to be seen and dealt with. Organizing my home, adding a little structure to my routines, and really thinking about the way my family functioned all helped me to seek peace and pursue it.

Now I want to challenge *you* to seek peace in your home. We're going to look at your stuff, your routines, your husband, and your children in the very light of Heaven. We'll listen for that spiritual clutter and we'll hold it up to scripture. You'll discern what you need to surrender and what requires action on your part.

The best way to start clearing out your spiritual clutter is by getting it out of your head and onto paper. Grab a notebook and pen, and get ready to jot down your thoughts as you read. At the end of the book, you'll find a study guide with a list of questions to help you. Challenge yourself to give some thought to your ways.

You can do this on your own, or ask a friend to read along with you. For more support, you can take this journey with several friends as a group study.[1] Decide how you're most likely to learn, grow, and stay motivated to clear out your spiritual clutter. Make the most of this process, and enjoy it!

Jesus Moms, get ready to build your home with both hands—it's time to get a bigger bucket.

---

1 If you're interested in taking this journey with friends, my *Building Your House* Group Bible Study curriculum is available for free through OrganizingJesusMoms.com. Yes, for free! Check it out!

Chapter 2

Your Stuff and Your Spirit

Whether you like things neat as a pin or usually couldn't care less about the mess, physical clutter takes up room in your spirit. Every crammed closet becomes an item on your infinite mental to-do list. Every messy pile is a "should-do" that keeps you from feeling like the great Jesus Mom you are.

It's difficult to concentrate when we're surrounded by clutter. We find ourselves thinking, *Wow, that's such a mess. I really should go through that. But when? And how? It's such a mess. I definitely need to go through that.* We're stuck on repeat, and nothing's getting accomplished.

When our belongings are difficult to access, it affects our choices. We put off tasks when we know we'll have to dig to find the necessary tools. When we can't find something, we shrug our shoulders and go without it, or buy it again. When an area is a mess anyway, we throw more things on the pile or shove them in the drawer, which just makes everything worse.

Possessions also drain our energy. Every item we own has to be taken care of. We have to find a place for it, clean it, and maintain it. It takes up space in our homes, minds, and schedules. The sheer amount of stuff we own can overwhelm us at times—having to deal with all of those belongings can make us feel *weary*.

Husbands and kids feel frazzled in the midst of clutter, too. Husbands are aggravated when they're looking for something and can't find it. Kids are overwhelmed with the constant stimulation of too many toys and too much stuff. And since we moms usually feel responsible for the amount of clutter we've accumulated, we're the most frustrated of all. With all of that angst flying around, family relationships suffer.

Other relationships may suffer as well. If we're embarrassed by our messy homes and cluttered spaces, we don't reciprocate our friends' invitations. We avoid hosting celebrations or out-of-town guests. Even our loved ones may misinterpret our excuses and begin to think we don't value our relationships with them.

Whew! All of that sounds terrible! Even if your house isn't *that* bad, there are probably still some areas that bog down your spirit when you think of them. Maybe some closets, cupboards,

[handwritten marginal note: Family]

[handwritten marginal note: Friends]

and drawers are hiding chaos. Perhaps some of your things are hard to access because they're buried in a pile or crammed in with too much other stuff. Maybe there's a whole room that makes you sigh when you pass through it (if you *can* pass through it).

No matter how organized—or disorganized—you are, physical clutter can cause clutter in your spirit. Out-of-control stuff affects your heart, mind, choices, energy level, family, and relationships. Jesus has more in mind for you than that. He wants you to live in a completely different kind of abundance!

Stay focused on the Lord!

The First Piece of Clutter to Toss

A true Christian perspective on home organization involves belongings, routines, husbands, kids, and most of all, allowing the Lord to use your home for Kingdom Work. These topics are all intertwined, so it's difficult (and possibly counter-productive) to work on one aspect of household management before you've considered them all.

You might be tempted to rush through the process so you can get organized, now. No matter what state your home is in, you need to let go of that false sense of urgency. When it comes to the state of our homes, we tend to be as dramatic as a six year old sweetie in a tiara. We think things like, *My house is such a disaster, I have to get organized!*

24

That's spiritual clutter, and you need to take a moment to clear it right out.

Your entire home is almost certainly not a disaster. You probably have plenty of great systems going, and you're certainly making it through each day. If nothing in your home changes this week or this month or even this year, no imminent disaster will strike.

There's no pressure here, no hurry. Don't go giving yourself even more spiritual clutter over "getting organized." In fact, I don't even like that phrase. It implies that "organized" is a place we can get to, a thing we can achieve, but it's not.

Your home isn't a problem to solve, it's a set of systems to be managed. As a Jesus Mom, you don't want to organize your household so you can "feel at peace." Instead, *you can choose to feel peaceful while you organize.*

You will build your home as a Jesus Mom, organizing your belongings in order to make your life easier. But first, we'll talk about the space your stuff takes up in His true realm—your heart.

Perspective change

Stuff Love

We're going to start our attack on your physical clutter with a touchy subject: how much you love your stuff. Even Christians find it far too easy to attach more importance to our possessions

25

than they deserve. Don't worry, I'm not going to make you throw it all away in a fit of minimalism. Nor will I tell you that if you truly love Jesus you'll get rid of it all. But I *do* want to challenge you to consider your belongings and what they mean to you, because I believe God calls us to do that in His Word.

Take the story of the Rich Young Ruler. And by "story," I don't mean fairytale or even parable, I mean a true story about an actual person. Whenever I read about him, I get the sense that he was a really nice guy—a lot like you and me. Faithful, rich by the standards of the world, and young!

In the tenth chapter of Mark, the rich young ruler approaches Jesus and asks Him how to get into Heaven. This seems like a deep and important question, but I have a feeling he was looking for reassurance more than an actual suggestion. He wanted Jesus to say, "You're already on your way—see you there!"

Like I said, the rich young ruler was a faithful, good guy. Our friend knew all of the commandments, and when Jesus listed a few for him—do not murder, do not steal, do not commit adultery, do not lie, honor your father and mother—you can practically hear the poor guy thinking, *Check...check...don't do that...that either...oh yes, I love my momma...I'm good!*

He proudly told Jesus that he had kept all of the commandments since he was a boy. Again, he's waiting for Jesus to say, "Well then, you're in!" Instead, Jesus looked at him and loved him.

26

Jesus looked at him and loved him.
"One thing you lack," he said. "Go, sell everything
you have and give to the poor, and you will have
treasure in heaven. Then come follow me."
At this the young man's face fell.
He went away sad, because he had great wealth.

Mark 10:21-22

Jesus wasn't being mean to our friend, or expecting too much. Jesus was loving him. He didn't say, "You have too much stuff to come with me," He said, "One thing you lack." What was that one thing? The Bible doesn't say, but I think it was this: the rich young ruler wasn't willing to go *all in* for Jesus.

Our Lord saw into his heart. He knew the rich young ruler's security and happiness were dependent upon his wealth rather than his faith. Jesus was challenging the young man to see it too, and change his ways.

As our friend walks out of the book of Mark, it's clear he didn't get it. This guy passed up the chance to follow Jesus—to live his life *with Jesus*—and my heart aches for him. I hope the rich young ruler became a rich middle-aged ruler and figured it out. I hope he heard the testimonies of the apostles and that his heart responded, that in the end he dethroned his possessions and chose to love the Lord with his whole heart.

I always hope this for him, and I hope it for us, as well. This story hits a little too close to home. We're blessed so richly that we can easily fall into the trap of relying upon our belongings for our sense of well-being.

Jesus looks at us and loves us. Jesus sees how dependent we are on our stuff when we should be depending on Him. He makes sure we have the things we need, and asks us not to worry about the rest. He challenges us to derive our security and contentment, not from our possessions, but from our Lord.

God may not be calling you into the kind of life where you need to let go of all of your possessions in order to serve Him. But through the story of the rich young ruler, He *is* calling you to realize how big a part of your life your stuff really is. He wants you to hold your belongings with open hands. He wants your treasure to lie with Him, because then your heart will be with Him as well. He's calling you to be *all in*.

Seeing Your Home from a Heavenly Perspective

Whether your home is monumentally messy or super structured, you see your belongings every day and do a certain amount of ignoring. You know what's frustrating you...and yet, it's still there. I want you to take a fresh look around your house and really *see* your things, to view your home through the eyes of Jesus.

First, try the Hundred-Years View. I had a friend in high school who was a big advocate of "hundred-years glasses." If I was upset about something—and being a teenage girl, I was frequently upset about something—she would advise me to look through my hundred-years glasses.

In one hundred years, I would be in Heaven with Jesus. *Will the thing I am upset about right now matter then—at all?* Of course, the answer to this question was almost always no! The same theory applies to our attachment to our belongings.

For a moment, use your hundred-years glasses to really see the possessions surrounding you. Eventually, you won't care about any of this stuff, because you're Heaven-bound! As Paul said to Timothy,

> But godliness with contentment is great gain.
> For we brought nothing into this world
> and we can take nothing out of it.
>
> *Timothy 6:6-7*

The true Hundred-Years View of your stuff is the image of your kids having to sort through it all. You may have faced these kinds of decisions after the passing of a parent, grandparent, or other relative. It's not fun. We Jesus Moms don't want to make more work for our kids in the future because we didn't deal with our belongings now.

29

Extra stuff is left behind

Jeff and I need to purge now!

Nor do we want to make more work for ourselves in the meantime! You don't want to spend the rest of your life wasting time and energy on things you don't even like that much. Instead, you can take a step toward godliness with contentment by making the choice to <u>simplify now</u>. *Project!*

Accordingly, the second view I'd like you to consider is the Near-Future View. Take a moment to picture how life would be for you, your husband, and your kids if you were living without excessive clutter or mess. Don't imagine unrealistic perfection, picture *real* life in your home—a life of intentional contentment. Look around your home and see it.

See relatively neat, orderly closets. Visualize functionally organized cupboards and drawers. Envision your home with clear, comfortable living spaces, and then imagine your family living there. Picture your space as lighter and more open—and feel how much lighter your spirit is as well. Talk about clearing out your spiritual clutter!

When you fully realize you can't take your possessions with you and imagine your family in a clutter free home, you gain a heavenly perspective on your belongings. You see your stuff for what it is: far more than you need. You don't have to have the scary-messy house of a true hoarder to toss aside the things in your way. We all have a lot of stuff—and I'm no exception.

Everything You Want in a Home—and More

After Spencer was born but while Karly was still a dream on the horizon, my little family lived in a sweet three-bedroom house. Travis set up a home office in the smallest bedroom, I had a scrapbooking desk in the family room, and all three of us could sit together at the little table in the kitchen. Our home was the perfect size for our family of three.

The only problem with that house was the distance between it and our extended family members. Thanks to the Lord, Travis found a new job and so we could move much closer to them. We began searching for the perfect house, the home in which we would raise Spencer and our future children. And not just that—we were choosing the home our kids would visit when they came home from college, the home in which we would eventually retire and play with our grandkids.

Even with those big plans in mind, it was a bit of a shock to transition from our small family-of-three house to a four-bedroom house complete with a dining room, a small home office, and a partially finished basement. I realized we didn't have nearly as much stuff as I'd thought! Entire rooms were devoid of furniture and two closets were empty. My beautifully organized sister-in-law Kristen asked me what I was going to *do* with all of that space.

The answer, of course, was fill it.

We've been living in this home for seven years now—a fantastic seven years—and let me tell you every closet is pretty full. The cabinet and drawer space is similarly occupied, and every room is well furnished. To be fair, we did add two extra family members whose belongings claimed two bedrooms, two closets, and some toy space in the main living areas.

But, we've added more possessions than can be accounted for by our growing family. Travis is definitely a "keeper" of stuff and Spencer seems to have inherited this gene. Both of my big guys dread our yearly garage sales—Travis has been known to hide things in the trunk of his car as if I would sell them without asking. During a routine check of Spencer's room, I'll discover caches of rocks, broken-off pencil erasers, and other boyhood treasures amid all those toys. Even I, a true "tosser" of stuff, have expanded my stores to include more scrapbooking tools, board games, and clothes.

In my head, I'm living a quiet, simple life with a minimal amount of stuff. No sweeping lawns or guest bedrooms. No fancy cars, *objets d'art*, or state-of-the-art entertainment systems. But sometimes I look around my home and shake my head at the sheer quantity of belongings we've accumulated.

In reality, Jesus Moms, *we're surrounded by so many material blessings that we're unable to count them.* We tend to accumulate as much stuff as our homes can hold, and that's OK. The problems start when we accumulate *more* stuff than our homes can handle.

Is the stuff in your home taking up space that should belong to your family members? Are you all getting frustrated with missing or hard-to-access belongings? Is taking care of all that stuff robbing you of time with your family, or the Lord? If so, you need to realize you could live with less.

And you know what? You might want to live with less, regardless.

How Much Stuff to Have: The 80% Rule

You're probably aware of the "simple living" movement, which espouses minimalism with an emphasis on environmentalism. I enjoy keeping up with new simple living ideas, but that isn't where my heart lies. I don't feel the need to get rid of most of my stuff and I won't ask you to, either. No, my heart lies in *simpler* living: comfortable, contented living with an emphasis on Christlikeness.

As Jesus Moms, our priorities are crystal clear: love the Lord, love our families, and love others. Loving stuff is not on the short list. If you're living outside of your means in terms of space, you know you should downsize your stuff. When we let go of our intrusive, excessive possessions, we can hold more tightly to Jesus and the people He's placed in our lives.

And even if you're thinking, *Well, my house is just the right size for our stuff*, I want you to consider downsizing, too. No matter how big or small your home is, I want to challenge you *not* to use all of your space. Instead, strive to abide by The 80% Rule.

You won't find this concept in organizing books where you're encouraged to "maximize your space" by filling every nook and cranny. Our Jesus Mom goal is to keep our homes at 80% capacity, with pockets of air in our closets, cabinets, and rooms. I'm challenging you to live in contentment with less, in a home where you're surrounded only with what you need and love. Your belongings should be *neatly contained and easily accessible* in your available space—which means you won't use it all.

Wait a minute, you're thinking, *If I have the space, why not fill it?* Well, for a simpler life. For less to take care of. So you can get things out and put them away with ease. So you have some extra space for your next big present influx (do I hear jingle bells?), the space to accommodate the ebb and flow of possessions in your life without needing to reorganize again and again. For more open space to *breathe*.

And to make sure that, unlike the rich young ruler, you're holding onto your belongings with open hands.

Right now, in your home, there are some things you're keeping around "just in case." Things you haven't touched in two years (or is it five?). Things you know you'll never, ever use again, but that bring back fond memories of people or events. Things you don't know what to do with, things you don't even like, things you don't want to take care of any more. These are the things that clutter up your home.

So here's the big question: Can you let these things go in order to make a simpler, less frustrating life for your family?

Say "yes," Jesus Moms, and let's get sorting!

Chapter 3

Clearing Out That Physical Clutter

I hope you didn't skip right to this chapter.

I know it's exciting! The desire to organize your stuff is probably why you started reading this book in the first place. You're all revved up and ready to organize, but I want you to do some more head and heart work with me first.

If you start to organize your stuff now, before taking your House Walk in Chapter 10, you'll likely end up going back to change what you've done. As Jesus Moms, we want well thought-out and prayed-over plans for our precious time and energy! Christ is on the throne and we're in no hurry.

What I'd like for you to do right now is to choose a space that needs organizing—a little space like a countertop, dresser, or small closet—and hold that space in your mind as you think through the organizing process with me. I want to help you overcome your counterproductive organizing habits and hang-ups before you truly begin! Then we'll add your routines and family members to the mix so you can make a big-picture plan for your Christ-centered household.

So while you're relaxing in your favorite reading chair and getting a few chocolate thumbprints on the pages, let's take a mental walk through the organizing process.

How To Tackle Any Small Space

Getting started can be the most difficult part of an organizing project, so make it as easy as possible! Hide your phone, shun your computer, and pump up the praise music. Choose a little reward to enjoy when you've finished. Get excited—you're taking on your stuff, and you will prevail!

Begin by praying over the space. Place your hands on or over it, dedicate it to the Lord, and ask Him to bless it. Ask for clarity and wisdom as you work. Ask for a heavenly view and a spirit of contentment as you consider your belongings. Finish by lifting your heart in thanksgiving for the blessings He's given you.

Now remove *everything* from the space you want to organize—since you've chosen a small space, this should be pretty quick work. If you have additional possessions you'd like to store in this space, now's the time to go get them and add them to the pile. (Often, storing like things together in one space is the most functional way to go.)

Take a moment to clean the empty areas. Dust the shelves, wipe the drawers, vacuum the carpet you haven't seen for a while. Take a deep breath and look at that beautiful space just waiting to hold your belongings in a neat, accessible way—or, if your goal is something like cleaning off a countertop, to never hold that random stuff again.

Then, turn around and look at the things you've taken out of the space. It may seem as though the stuff grew and multiplied while your back was turned (the sci-fi nerd in me is picturing tribbles). No worries. You're going to tackle it with a Quick Sort, dividing your big, haphazard pile into smaller, meaningful piles.

Try to keep a nice, efficient pace going during this part of the process—no dawdling. The Quick Sort isn't a time for deep thought, just easy work. Sing along with that praise music as you pick up each item and quickly place it in the correct pile.

- The Keep Pile: The Keep Pile is easy—it's for the items you either *need* or *love,* as in totally adore. There shouldn't be a second's hesitation when you put something in the Keep Pile.

- **The Elsewhere Pile:** This pile is similar; it's for the "keep" stuff that doesn't belong in that particular space. Don't stop sorting to put an item away! You'll get distracted and lose your momentum—remember, this is a Quick Sort and that's what the Elsewhere Pile is for!

- **The Maybe Pile:** If you're hesitating at all, then it goes in the Maybe Pile. This is for something you might want to keep...but you're just not sure. Don't spend time mulling over it during the Quick Sort. Just call it a "maybe" and keep going.

- **The Give Away Pile:** This is the place for the things you'd like to donate, sell in a garage sale, or unload online through sites like eBay, craigslist, or Freecycle. Someone else will need it or love it—but you know that you don't. Let God bless other people with these items!

- **The Toss Pile:** Simply put, these things aren't good enough for anybody. (Depending on what you're sorting, you may want to make a Recycle Pile instead.)

You should feel really good about adding to those last two piles. You're holding your belongings loosely and making room for the things that matter to you. You won't have to take care of that stuff or find space for it any more. You're placing some spiritual clutter in those piles, as well!

The Maybe Pile

After you've done your Quick Sort, it's time to turn your attention to the Maybe Pile. Every item in your Maybe Pile needs to be sorted into one of the other four piles. This round will probably be a little more difficult.

Jesus Moms, if you put an item in the Maybe Pile, you probably don't need it or totally love it—so you should seriously consider letting it go. Deep down, you know when an item isn't right for you and your family. If you haven't used it in a year or two, or if it's out of date, damaged, or unusable in a practical way, then out it goes.[1]

If you spent too much on a certain item (or simply never used it), don't let the spiritual clutter of guilt crowd out your common sense! You may be tempted to try to correct your mistake by keeping the item—"to get more use out of it"—but instead its very presence will remind you of your misstep. Instead, lift it up to the Lord. He'll forgive you that misjudgment and you can forgive yourself. He can redeem your mistake by using that item for the good in someone else's life, so let it go.

In fact, don't keep anything just to keep it, especially if

---

1 When you're ready to get in there and organize an area, open up to Appendix A, "A Step-by-Step Guide for Sorting Through Any Space." It's a concise summary of the process and contains a complete list of questions to ponder as you're sorting through your Maybe Pile.

you're squeezing it in or having to find new, bigger ways to store it. There's a parable in Luke 12 about a man who goes so far as to tear down his barns and build bigger ones, just to hold his stuff—it's called "The Parable of the Rich Fool." We don't want to be that fool any more than we want to be the foolish woman in Proverbs 14:1!

Instead, choose to be the wise Proverbs 14 Woman and build your house with both hands. Your home isn't built with stuff, it's built with the love of Jesus. He's blessed you with an abundance of things, but you're holding them loosely. You have a certain amount of space for your belongings, and you've decided not to fill it to the brim. Remember your 80% goal. If you don't need it or really love it, then let it go.

Of course, you don't *have* to get rid of everything in your Maybe Pile. If you go at it with the mindset that you need to purge your home of everything that isn't strictly necessary, then you'll resist and eventually sabotage your own efforts. Just as you don't want to keep for the sake of keeping, you don't need to toss for the sake of tossing. Wise King Solomon wrote that there's

...A time to search and a time to give up,
a time to keep and a time to throw away...

Ecclesiastes 3:6

You're a capable, Jesus-loving Proverbs 14 Woman, so listen to your mind's knowledge and your heart's whisper. There are plenty of things in your Maybe Pile that you may deem functional or important after a moment's thought. Even if you don't *love* an object, you may decide that really liking it is a fine reason to keep it.

Also, now that you've seen and touched everything that was in your space, you have a better sense of what you'd like to keep there. You may have plenty of room for some of your Maybe Pile items in the available 80% of your space. That's fine, *as long as you're making a decision to keep those things, not just resisting the urge to let them go.*

Jesus Moms, you're in control of your stuff. You get to choose. Challenge yourself to make more room for you and your family. Clear the clutter out of your home and your spirit...but don't make yourself cry.

A Sentimental Journey

While we're uncluttering our spirits, let's address the emotional currency that often has nothing to do with an item's selling price. God created us with hearts full of love, and sometimes that love spills over onto objects. When we hold cherished possessions, memories flood in and we're reminded of people or places we hold dear. Despite being a tosser by nature, I know all about sentimental value.

I once had a sentimental attachment to a 3-hole punch. Yes, a 3-hole punch. It's a long story, but that 3-hole punch helped Travis and me move from "just friends" to "dating." And every nerdy, organized girl loves her 3-hole punch! I used mine to punch three holes into both my senior thesis and my very first lesson plans as Miss Kelley, Math Teacher Extraordinaire. I even used it to compile my wedding binder (oh yes, I had a wedding binder, didn't everyone?).

Then one of my high school math students, a big, football-playing senior named Shawn, punched with a little too much gusto. I heard the sound of the spring as it sprung and the crunch of bending metal. Shawn looked up at me (actually he looked down at me) and said, "Dude, I think I broke it."

I'm ashamed to admit that tears actually welled in my eyes. The poor kid said, "Whoa, Mrs. Upton, I'll get you a new one!"

I quickly replied, "Oh no, it's not a big deal, Shawn. Forget about it." But then I turned away and cradled my little hole punch forlornly.

I took it home and tried to fix it, to no avail. I kept it for about a year, hoping that I would think of a way to get it working again or that it would spontaneously repair itself. I didn't, and it didn't. I finally threw it away, but I still remember it fondly. And I'm not even that sentimental.

My mom, a completely amazing Jesus Mom, is *very* sentimental about belongings. She especially treasures things that used to belong to family members, many of whom passed away long before she had the chance to meet them. This is something I don't really get, but she did manage to pass on a mild case of Family Member Belonging Attachment to me.

A few years ago my Great Aunt Donna passed away, and shortly thereafter my Great Uncle Gerald joined her in Heaven. Our entire extended family met at their home to see if we'd like to keep any of their belongings. It was a sad occasion, but I enjoyed being with my cousins and reminiscing about the times we'd spent in Uncle Gerald and Aunt Donna's home.

I chose several things to remind me of them. I filled an entire box with holiday decorations that sweetly brought to mind the Christmas Eve gatherings they'd hosted. I also selected a few cookbooks with handwritten notes inside them, four sets of retro glass snack trays with punch glasses, a complete set of silver, and several other treasures. To cap it all off, I took the large set of family china that none of my siblings or cousins seemed to want—complete service for twelve, with several sizeable serving pieces including a soup tureen. Before I knew it, I'd filled the trunk of my car and most of the backseat with boxes of stuff.

I stood there for a moment, looking incredulously at my rapidly filling car. *I can't believe I'm taking home all of this stuff.*

What will Travis say? Where am I going to put it all? Then my sweet momma walked up behind me, looked at the very same car, and asked, "Is that all you're taking?!" (She found a few more things for me, no worries.)

I'm sharing these two stories so you'll know that I truly understand the Maybe Pile quandary. If I can be attached to a 3-hole punch, then anyone can be sentimentally attached to anything. And if my momma, who loves her some Jesus, can be so sentimentally attached to mere possessions, then even the strongest Jesus Mom can have a hard time letting go of belongings that hold emotional meaning for her.

Of course, we can choose to keep sentimental things…as long as they're filling our hearts with joy, not clutter.

Letting Go of the Good So You Can Enjoy the Best

Under my bed, I have a shoebox of love notes, ticket stubs, anniversary cards, and other mementos that represent my love for Travis. I also have a shoebox containing special keepsakes from dear friends and family members, and a "Mommy" box with special drawings and Mother's Day cards from my kids. Those three boxes of blessings are there for me to enjoy whenever I wish.

When I'm immersed in their contents, I feel surrounded by the love of my family, my friends, and the Lord. Sentimental things like these are inherently good—in small doses. But if we keep *all* of that stuff, we won't be able to enjoy any of it.

While a shoebox of mementoes under your bed can give you a happy hour down memory lane, stacks of huge plastic tubs in your basement will never be looked at again. You won't bother wading through daunting amounts of memorabilia, and you wouldn't get the same warm fuzzy feelings if you did. You'd be too busy taking random objects out of the boxes and thinking, *now what is this again?*

The key to sorting through sentimental items is to keep the things that are extraordinarily special and let the rest go. This applies to gifts from loved ones, greeting cards, souvenirs from trips, and even (prepare for this one, moms) your child's artwork and schoolwork.

Despite what we may imagine, our kids won't want to sit and look through it all with us someday. Twenty minutes into the first box labeled "Preschool," even the most sentimental grown-up kid will be ready to run. In the end, keeping all of those papers is no better than throwing them all away.

Instead, let's determine to fully appreciate those great pieces of art and A+ papers *now*. Display them on the fridge or the doors of their bedrooms. I hang my children's artwork near the door to our garage so we get that home-sweet-home feeling when we walk inside. My friend Christy plasters the walls of her basement stairwell with her kids' artwork so that it looks like really fun wallpaper. Pinterest is full of creative, stylish ways to display kids' masterpieces.

But to maintain these displays effectively, you have to take one thing down as you put a new one up. You've fully enjoyed the one you're removing, so you can let it go. Simply toss it, or send it on to a grandparent or cousin—someone who'll enjoy a surprise in the mail but won't have any problem throwing it away later. (We often send the kids' Sunday school creations to the child we sponsor in the Dominican Republic.) For a large piece of artwork or a bulkier item like a science project, try taking a picture of your child holding it—that sweet smile of pride is the best part anyway.

I do have one large tub of "keepers" for each child slowly filling with important treasures. I only include the best items and make sure to write the pertinent information on the backs. Ten years from now, I won't remember that Karly had just turned five when she drew the picture of us walking through Candyland. Without the reminder, I probably won't even remember it's supposed to *be* Candyland! When I go through her tub someday (probably in preparation for her high school graduation party), rediscovering those things will be half the fun.

When we're selective about our "keepers," everything we save can be a source of joy!

Collecting Joy

Of course, we all collect things besides our kids' creations. Full disclosure: books are my collecting downfall. Those brightly colored spines arranged on my shelves, and the feel of the pages between my fingers, fill me with happiness. I love paper and I do love my books.

However, the shelves on which I store my books are the same shelves that hold my scrapbooks. As time marches on and more and more precious scrapbooks fill the space, some of the books have got to go. If it's a choice between storing a scrapbook filled with family pictures and storing an old book-club book, there's really no competition. Yet still my heart resists, especially if it's a hardback!

The bottom line about the book is this: I'll never read it again. I'm keeping it just to have it in my collection, and I'm running out of room. Someone else can read it and enjoy it. I need to let it go, and several of my other books, too—then I'll treat myself to some scrapbooking time (and a little chocolate)!

Like me, you might be tempted to overlook your collections of stuff when you take your House Walk and it's time to sort. You know, ordinary things like books, movies, CDs, games, craft supplies, cookbooks, kitchen gadgets, toys, and clothing items like t-shirts.[2] They all

---

2 For help with toys and clothes specifically, check out "The Toy Challenge" and "The Closet Clean-Out" articles on OrganizingJesusMoms.com.

go together and you tend to see them as one thing. You've been collecting them forever...you can't break up the set.

Well, you can if you're running out of room, or spending an inordinate amount of time taking care of them. When sorting through an informal collection, consider each item on an individual basis, and if in doubt, let it go. In your head, the individual elements are simply part of the larger group anyway; you almost certainly won't miss the ones you weed out. When you let them go, you free up space and time for the things you need and love.

Even your most beloved collection of special objects can overwhelm your living space, in which case it's giving you spiritual clutter. Collections are only worthy of your space if each piece brings you joy. Pick your very favorite items and put them on display, or actually put them into use so you'll enjoy them every day! Then let go of the rest.

While you're sorting, you may realize you've outgrown the entire collection (hey, you don't even like those things any more!), so you can let go of the whole kit and caboodle. If you're holding on to a collection because you're waiting for it to be valuable someday, protect your living space by storing the group in an out-of-the-way place like your attic or basement.

Then there are those individual sentimental items scattered throughout your home. You'll stumble across them as you're sorting through your spaces, and many will end up in your Maybe Pile.

You may be holding onto gifts from friends or family members, or gifts from your husband which you've never really enjoyed, but all of which hold precious memories of the giver. Or perhaps you're allowing essentially worthless vacation souvenirs to clutter up your shelves because thinking of the trip makes you smile.

You *can* let these things go without letting go of the memories. If an item reminds you of a special event, a funny story, a wonderful trip, or a beloved person, try journaling about that item and the memories it evokes in you.[3] You may even want to take a picture of the item and start a scrapbook—it will take up less space in your home, yet still fill your heart with joy!

When it's time to place a sentimental item in the Give Away or Toss piles, you can take a moment to feel the love. That object was really special to someone once—maybe you—but it's fulfilled its purpose and it's time to let it go. Thank the Lord for the joy it's given you, then hold on to Jesus and remember this: *you don't have to have the specific item in your hands in order to feel the love it represents in your heart.*

Love is a gift from God and He is not contained by things. You're not either.

---

3 To help you get started writing about these items, I've written an article called "Joyful Journaling" on OrganizingJesusMoms.com.

Chapter 4

Storing Your Stuff

Let's end our sentimental journey and get back to the process of organizing your space. You've distributed your Maybe Pile items into the Keep, Elsewhere, Give Away, and Toss piles. You've got those lovely piles in front of you and a clean, ready-to-go empty space behind you. The sorting is over and you did it with Jesus in mind!

Take out the Toss and Recycle piles immediately. Next, box up the things in your Give Away pile. If you plan to donate them, put the boxes in your car so you can drop them off at your earliest convenience. If you prefer to list the items online or sell them at your garage sale, price your things and label the boxes. Be sure to write any associated to-do items in your planner and mark your family calendar with any related dates.

Next, distribute the Elsewhere Pile items through the rest of your house like a happy fairy spreading joyful order—but don't simply sprinkle them around! If you're not quite sure where to put something, it's awfully tempting just to stick it somewhere. But without a place to call home, it'll end up back in the space you just cleared out. Better to be intentional and decide where it should reside!

If you're clearing off an open space like a kitchen counter or your dining room table, then this is the end of the process. You've cleared the physical clutter out of the space and the correlated spiritual clutter out of your heart! You may want to put something pretty there, like a vase of flowers or a framed Bible verse, so you won't be tempted to let things accumulate there again. A little beauty can help you enjoy that space *and* keep it clutter free.

If you do have a Keep Pile, then you're ready to put those items back where they belong. You may want to take a moment to dust or wipe off each belonging—and be thankful for these small blessings! You need them, you love them, and you've made the choice to store and maintain them.

Jesus Moms, get ready to store everything in your Keep Pile in a neat, accessible way. Talk about building your house for your Lord and your family—here comes the fun part!

Pretty Organizing (It's Pretty Overrated)

I know some of you may not think of this as the "fun part." Maybe for you, sorting was a piece of cake compared to organizing what's left. *This* might be the difficult, overwhelming part. What if you don't know how to do it the right way?

Well, I would argue that there is no wrong way.

As the author of a book about organization, I should have picture-perfect storage spaces, right? My cupboards should be immaculate, my drawers should all be neatly divided, and my closets should be filled with fabulously color-coded boxes. My label maker should have died from heat exhaustion.

Actually, most of my storage spaces aren't very pretty and boast nary a label. For one thing, I'm too frugal to buy the beautiful boxes and such that would make my spaces look magazine-worthy. And if I *did* buy those beautiful boxes, the stuff of life would come in and go out and my systems would have to change anyway. I'd end up with nonmatching boxes, and that's no fun.

Also, I live in a home with four other people and none of them are inclined to spend time reading my labels or fitting everything into my beautiful systems "just so." In fact, I'm not inclined to spend my time that way either! I want to be able to put things away and find them again with as little fuss as possible.

For Jesus Moms, household organization isn't about having

gorgeous, photogenic closets. It's certainly not about keeping all of your things in alphabetical order or another equally rigid system. It's about storing your stuff in a way that's *functional*, a way that works for you and your family—not anyone else's.

There's a lot of media out there purporting to show us what it means to be organized, never more than now. Bloggers and pinners offer a plethora of organizational ideas for us to discover with just a few keystrokes. As we compare these posed images to our very real homes, "I should" and "I want" thoughts can clutter our spirits.

In reality, those pretty pictures of "organized" spaces are often unrealistic and inefficient. If you're using clear storage containers, why tape pictures of the contents to the outside? Why hang your clothes in rainbow order? (And if you do, how do you classify a red and blue plaid skirt?) Unless you have ten kids, you probably don't need an entire wall for a "command center"—what a hassle it must be to keep that up to date.

In fact, I believe that most of these organizing "tips" are purely organization for organization's sake, and that many "organizational tools" serve only to frustrate the user. I'm especially mystified by those special containers for dry food items, like the plastic ones made for cereal. In my house, cereal is inhaled. If I transferred our cereal in and out of plastic tubs, washing and drying them every time, I'd make myself crazy.

I do understand the urge to make spaces pretty. I just love how my craft space is organized—it's so functional and it's the prettiest organizing I've ever done! But do you know how many people have walked in my door and said, "Shannon, can I see your beautifully organized craft supplies?" That would be none. (Although I did make my mom, my sister, and a couple of my friends admire it with me for a few happy moments.)

Pretty can be fun. Pretty can be joyful! But pretty should not be done simply to impress others, nor should it place stress on your family, time, or budget. And most of all, pretty should never be less than completely functional.

Prevailing Over Perfectionism

If you're the kind of mom who treasures her cereal containers, loves her rainbow-beautiful closet, or joyfully does any of the other things I just mentioned, please know that I'm not judging you. We all have different comfort levels when it comes to home organization. Every mom needs to choose organizing systems that her family can actually live with and maintain properly.

Type-A mommies like me take organizing ideals to heart. We overorganize, arranging things in such structured ways that our families are unable to maintain our systems. We end up shoving things into our overcomplicated spaces, figuring we'll get to them later...and then we have to "reorganize." We clutter our spirits with our failed methods and wasted efforts, rather than loosening up and adjusting to our families. We need to embrace the fact that if it really works, it's better than "perfect!"

Moms who are uncomfortable with a lot of structure can also fall victim to perfectionistic organizing ideals. These "Unstructured Moms" use unrealistic standards as a way to keep the whole idea at an arm's length—if they can't keep their belongings in perfect order, then they might as well not even try. Then they clutter up their spirits by struggling to find what they want in the mess. They need to create loosely structured systems that will really work for them.

Plenty of moms in the middle of this spectrum carry around a perfectionistic ideal of organizing as well, and would claim not to be organized if anyone asked them. These moms are probably organized in a very functional way and have numerous great systems. They need to appreciate what's really working—and stay open to tweaking what isn't.

Jesus Moms, our Lord isn't calling us to be "perfect" homemakers. He's calling us to be good stewards of our blessings—and you can do that no matter how much structure you feel comfortable employing in your home. The key to functional organizing is deciding just how organized is "organized enough" to satisfy your heart and keep your household running smoothly.

Each time you set up an organizational system, ask yourself this: what's the *least* amount of structure that will make our things the *most* accessible? That's the organizing standard that will clear the clutter out of your spirit!

Container Shopping

When you set aside perfectionism to look realistically at your Keep Pile and the awaiting space, you may realize that your original storage system was fine. The items in your Keep Pile may fit neatly and with room to spare, now that you're not trying to cram so much stuff into the space. You might be able to put it right back, pretty much as it was. Hooray!

But even with a heart determined to keep things simple, sometimes you'll decide that putting your belongings back as they were isn't the way to go. If you need to update your storage system in order to keep your things neat and accessible, then you may need to buy some containers or other organizational products. (Even better, when you do your House Walk in Chapter 10, you may repurpose things you already own.)

Notice this is the *last* step you take when you organize a space. Don't be fooled into preemptively buying those great containers at the store before you begin sorting, even if they're on sale. They probably won't fit into your space—or your stuff won't fit into them the way you'd like. No container is cost-effective if it's not exactly what you need and thus clutters your spirit for the next ten years!

Even expensive, super cute containers may not be practical—just picture yourself facing a stack of trendily decorated boxes and realizing the item you need is in the bottom one. Also, many adorable containers won't keep your things clean. Kitchen utensils in cute counter-top jars end up splattered with batter. Items in pretty baskets get dusty, and open bins for toys usually collect more than just toys (*ick*).

Instead, determine to be a smart container shopper. Wait until you're done sorting so you know exactly what things need to be contained. Take the time to visualize how you'd like to access your things. Make a list of what you need and take a picture of your Keep Pile with you to the store.

Take a moment to measure your space so you'll know which containers will fit. Be sure to measure the entry and exit dimensions, like the frames that partially block doorways, cabinets, and drawers. Many storage containers have measurements printed right on their labels, but take your tape measure to the store with you just in case.

And keep an open mind—you can get some great storage ideas just by looking around at what the store (or your basement) has to offer. You may come up with new organizing ideas using products you didn't know existed, or products intended for other purposes. You *can* create wonderful, unique systems for your family!

Hopefully, you'll uncover more specific ideas about what to buy—and what not to buy—as we take a deeper look at how to organize your things. The following two general organizing theories can help you plan your neat and accessible systems.

Loose Genre Organization

One of the best ways to organize your things is by type, keeping like things together in general groups. I call this Loose Genre Organization. By giving yourself a general framework, you can find your belongings easily and replace them even more quickly.

For example, recipe card boxes are organized this way. They have sections for appetizers, main courses, desserts, and beverages, but the individual recipes don't have specific spots. The recipes are easy to find within their sections, and you can just toss them in the general category when you put them away.

When you look around with Loose Genre Organization in mind, you might discover things spread all over your home that should be grouped together. By storing them in one place, you'll always know where to find them and where to put them away. (One example is placing your family's shoes in a basket by the door.)

Also, some of your collections of stuff will have natural divisions, so you can store these items in a very functional way. You might want to arrange your personal library by genres such as fiction, self-help, faith, and children's books. You can group your clothes by types: tops, pants, church or work clothes, sweaters, and accessories. You probably already have your kids' possessions grouped this way, with doll clothes in one box, Legos in another, and sporting equipment in a certain area of your garage.

Your husband and kids will love this kind of organization. After you explain the groupings to them, they'll be better able to find what they're looking for without asking you. And when they learn they don't have to put things back in *exactly* the same place—just in there with the others—they'll be much more likely to put them away. So will you! You'll be able to keep your belongings organized without a lot of hassle or spiritual clutter.

Point of Use Organization

Another great way to keep your things accessible is to store them exactly where they're actually used. This sounds easier than it really is! The rooms that see the most action often have less storage than we'd like. And then there are those items that you think of as "belonging" in a certain area when you actually use them in a different area altogether.

Let's say your mother always kept her ironing board in her bedroom closet, so that's where you keep yours. It does make a certain amount of sense: the ironing board is with your clothes, after all, and there's probably a nice flat wall in your closet to lean it up against. However, you probably don't iron in or next to your clothes closet.

If you're like me, you fight that pressing boredom by ironing in front of the TV. So you have to go upstairs to get your ironing board, carry it downstairs, and return it when you're done. Honestly, this small hassle would be enough to make me procrastinate this chore (you know, even more than I already do).

If you iron in your family room, then that's the best place to store your ironing board. You may have to be creative! You could keep it under or behind your couch. If that's not feasible, keep it in a nearby closet or laundry room. Above all, you need to get that ironing board—and everything else—at its point of use.

Toys are a must for Point of Use Organizing. For example, dominoes are great for hand-eye coordination but aren't any fun on carpet, so you should keep them in a room with hard flooring. If your kids are only allowed to play with Play-Doh on the kitchen table, then don't store it in their bedrooms where the temptation may be too great (ahh, Play-Doh smashed in the rug!). If you want your big kids to use their electronics where you can supervise them, devise a "charging station" in your kitchen.

61

Point of Use Organization can also apply to organizing your shelving areas and cabinets, although in that case it can become a "time of use" decision. Your everyday items should be the easiest to access, stored between eye-level and knee-level. Medium-high or very low-level storage should contain things you use only once or twice a month.

High-level shelving should contain those items you only use a few times a year. If it's a holiday-related item, consider storing it in your basement or attic with your seasonal decorations. Protect your prime real estate—keep the part of the house you really live in at 80% capacity!

The storage areas in each room should only hold the things you actually use there. If a certain room is space-challenged, take a good look around. Perhaps some of the things cluttering up the room don't need to be there. You can create more living space by moving those things to their actual point of use.

Using Loose Genre and Point of Use Organization, you'll organize all of your belongings in a way that clears out your spiritual clutter and makes room for peace—well, at least until you get more stuff, right?

What To Do with the New Stuff

Even when all of your belongings are neatly organized,

new possessions flow into your home every time you shop—not to mention the tidal wave that hits your organizational systems on birthdays and holidays. You may have to reorganize, but that should be a last resort for big life changes like a move or the addition of a new family member. Instead, decide in advance how you'll deal with all that new stuff.

Hopefully, as you were sorting, you followed The 80% Rule. If so, you have some room to accommodate a few more related things in your functionally organized spaces. But rather than adding belongings until you need to sort them all again, try replacement—take something out for every new thing you put in.

Most items you purchase or receive can replace something you already have. Replace instead of collect when it comes to things like books, DVDs, or kitchen gadgets. Consider replacing your clothing—when you buy a new pair of jeans, let go of an old pair you never wear anyway. And use replacement to teach your kids about living with less (new toy in means old toy out).

Another way to clear some space is to walk through your house once or twice a year with a laundry basket on your hip, scanning each room, closet, cupboard, and drawer for items to let go. You could add this quick scan to your monthly lists of tasks for December and June—December because it's right before Christmas, when you'll be needing a little more space, and June because it's before your neighborhood garage sale.

Doing a walk-through like this shouldn't take long, certainly no more than an hour. You're not organizing anything or spending time with each object, you're just looking for unwanted stuff. You'll probably stumble across things you *almost* let go the last time you organized—those Maybe Pile quandaries. If you haven't thought of them since the sort and you know you're not likely to use them again, toss them in the basket. (It can be a lot easier to clear out these items after a little time has passed!)

Your quick scan will leave empty pockets of air in your space—and that's the goal. Don't feel like you need to reorganize to make it look neater. You'll fill the holes eventually, and in the meantime you're better off not taking care of things you don't really want. Price these gleaned items for your garage sale, list them online, or donate them immediately. (Don't forget to write down any associated to-do items in your planner.)

Of course, the best way to keep your house clutter free is to avoid buying unnecessary stuff. When you're thinking about buying any item less vital than toilet paper, ask yourself: Do I *love* it, or just like it? Am I buying it because it's a "good deal?" Where will I keep it? If you're on the fence about a purchase, remember you can always put the item on your Christmas list.

If spending is an issue for you, try prayerfully asking, *Lord, will this purchase be a good use of Your financial blessings?* When you challenge yourself to reduce your spending, you'll reduce the clutter in your home, spirit, *and* credit card bills. You don't need *things* to be happy—in fact, you may be happier without them.

Finding Contentment with Your Portion

Jesus Moms know that life isn't about stuff. Our belongings aren't a security blanket; our possessions do not make us happy. We don't need to buy the next thing on our wish lists. We're not just consumers, we're consumed by the love of Jesus Christ.

Jesus Moms view our things, not as necessities to which we're entitled, nor as burdens we have to maintain, but as blessings for which our hearts are so very thankful. As David said,

> Lord, you have assigned me my portion and my cup;
> you have made my lot secure.
> The boundary lines have fallen for me in pleasant places;
> surely I have a delightful inheritance.
>
> *Psalm 16:5-6*

When we pause to consider our blessings, we're intentionally drinking the portion the Lord has given us from the cup He has assigned. He's blessed us with our husbands, our children, our belongings, our very *salvation*, and made our lot secure in Him. He gives us exactly what we need, and for us, the boundary lines fall in pleasant places. Jesus Moms, we have a delightful inheritance.

Organizing your home is a wonderful way to fulfill your calling as a Jesus Mom and find that intentional contentment. You can decide how important—or unimportant—your belongings are and make decisions accordingly. You can maintain a functionally organized home with a little room to spare. You can lead the way for your husband and kids, helping them live contented lives in a home free of unnecessary clutter.

With your heart and attitude, you can create a spirit of purpose and peace for your family. With your hands, you can create order and functionality that will mean almost as much to them. You can make your home into a refuge, a safe place, a haven for your husband and kids, and for yourself.

In a home where you're surrounded only by the things you need and love, your thoughts will be able to drift away from the *stuff* you need to take care of so you can enjoy the *people* you're blessed to care for—your husband and children. You'll be closer to them and closer to the Lord, and no amount of stuff will be able to get in your way.

Build this out in a discussion

Handwritten notes (margins):

3 Jul 18

At this point in time my day to day feels crazy like I just can't catch up. As to press towards my calling it gets worse.

This may just be God allowing me to feel so anxious that women feel we are stir time. & I don't know what they are going through how can I relate & help. An organizing mom must be centered around God, our family & our purpose. Not what the world says

Chapter 5

Creating Peace with Routines

I love ads from the 1950s and 60s, the ones in which women have idyllic homes and families. They bake cakes from scratch in flattering, frilly aprons and gracefully vacuum in high heels. Their kids are purely adorable, their husbands kiss them when they get home from work, and their homes are organized to perfection. Life would be sweet in a home like that. Wouldn't it?

It's all too easy to believe that as soon as our belongings are beautifully organized, life will be smooth sailing. All of the organizing media out there seems to promise us that with our things in place, the rest of our lives will fall in line. But deep down, we know better.

Household management is a challenge no matter how orga-

Handwritten note (bottom): & We set an expectation that is not realistic.

67

nized our closets are.[1] In this chapter, we're going to tackle your routines. Within them are those everyday moments that *always* seem to go the wrong way. Those times of day when you know there's going to be trouble, and you regularly find yourself praying for strength!

Part of what charms us about that late-50s-early-60s era is the sense of consistency. In black and white or freshly colorized sitcoms, the women do the same things in the same way every day. The families we're watching may have some entertaining adventures, but by the end of the episode they're having dinner together as a family or kissing their kids' foreheads as they tuck them into bed.

We can achieve that appealing sense of structure and security in our homes by creating and maintaining routines for our families. Well thought-out routines can keep you moving smoothly from one part of your day to the next. Prayed-over routines will infuse your household with a special atmosphere of peace.

Which is not the same thing as boredom.

Q's
1. Do I ever pray over my routines?
2. Are my priorities set with God / Family in mind.

---

1 In fact, the foundation of fantastic household management is intentional time management. I'd love for you to get a planner and create a personalized system with the help of my first *Organizing You* book and the free printable planner pages on OrganizingJesusMoms.com!

Routine Resistance

Routine organizing is anything but routine! God made us all with different tolerances for structure, systems, and messes. As I've mentioned (maybe a couple of times), you need to find the level of organization that works for *you*, and this includes developing personalized routines. However, Jesus Moms of all types find themselves resisting this kind of organization.

Type-A moms like me usually love routines. However, we have the tendency to impose too much structure on our families, trying in vain to force them to follow our rules. After all, our highly considered, logical procedures should work—our husbands and kids should fall in line!—so we fail to think of practical ways to change and improve our routines.

On the other end of the spectrum, the Unstructured Moms make a routine out of not having one. In their homes, you never know what's going to come next. Naps are optional, mealtimes fluctuate, and bedtimes vary. Unstructured Moms may thrive in this kind of atmosphere, but they have to watch out—their husbands and kids may not. And even the most relaxed mom gets frazzled and overwhelmed when the same things go wrong again and again.

These moms strongly resist creating routines. They think they don't want them (because routines are restrictive and boring), or they can't have them (because routines are for those organized people), but neither of these things is true. If you're holding onto either of these assumptions, consider this: you *do* have routines, they're just ineffectual ones!

I suspect that moms in the middle of the organizational spectrum struggle most with ineffective routines. They have that enviable semi-organized, go-with-the-flow spirit which serves them well in so many areas of their lives—but when it comes to routines, going with the flow can be a detriment.

Moms-in-the-Middle with a bad routine tend to wait for things to get better on their own. *Well, it's taking me ninety minutes to tuck him in right now. It's exhausting, and I miss hanging out with my husband at night...but it's just a phase.* Yes, it is just a phase—her little one won't require marathon tuck-ins when he's fifteen years old—but bad routines like this one are incredibly frustrating and stressful in the meantime.

In I Corinthians 14, Paul wrote to new believers about orderly worship. He instructed them not to speak over each other, but to do everything with the goal of building up the church. He tells us in verse 33 that our God is not a God of disorder, but of peace. Then he closes the section with this:

Amen! But everything should be done in a fitting and orderly way.

I Corinthians 14:40

Our God of peace created us to enjoy order—we're made in His image. No matter where you are on the structure spectrum, you'll benefit from well-designed routines. Just as orderly worship builds up the church, orderly homes build up the family. Fitting and orderly routines can give consistency to your home and peace to your heart.

[handwritten annotation: Order brings peace & security to our families. Kids thrive and feel loved w/ structure.]

Avoiding the Little Potholes in the Great Road of Life

Each morning, you have a general picture of how your day will go. With the love of Jesus and your family in your heart, you're probably happy to get things rolling. Your spirit is willing even if, like me, your flesh is weak. (Have I mentioned that I'm not a morning person?)

However, you may anticipate one or two typical daytime happenings that make staying in bed seem more tempting. You dread those parts of your day that are consistent all right—consistently stressful. These bumps in your road can ruin your happy momentum and clutter your spirit.

Maybe you tend to run late in the morning, so your days start under a dark cloud. Or you dread going anywhere because it's so hard to get out of the house. Perhaps mealtimes are a struggle, homework is a hassle, or bedtimes are a battle and you're losing the fight. Kids: 948—Mom: 0.

For me, it can be that horrible time right around 5:00 p.m. You know, when we're trying to make dinner, big kids need help with homework, and little kids are wound up and hungry. If I'm not careful, I find myself waiting desperately for my husband to get home and *help me out*. If you work outside the home, you may return to this five o'clock chaos on a daily basis, and if you're a mom of teens, you probably have an eye on the clock because you need to chauffer someone to practice soon!

Even Jesus Moms have a hard time staying cheerful, patient, and thankful when we're just plain aggravated. When the same issues repeatedly trip us up, our irritation is nearly instantaneous. We think, *I hate this time of day, why is it so hard?* or, *I can't believe we're doing this AGAIN.*

Our tendency is to push through it and go on to the next thing, hoping it will go better tomorrow. Or we lash out at our family members in frustration. In those stressful moments, it's difficult to stop and figure out what's going wrong.

Note! Part of building your home with both hands is figuring out how you might inadvertently be tearing it down. No single part of your day should persistently annoy you or involve a stressful battle. A day in the life of your family is actually a set of routines, some great and some not so great, one right after the other. When you identify the not-so-great parts, you can make them better.

Try choosing an upcoming day, one that promises to be "typical" for your family, and intentionally observe how you move through it. Pinpoint what parts of your day tend to frustrate you, your husband, or your kids—those times that cause you spiritual clutter. Then you can smooth over these rough spots with an organized routine.

All in Good Time

Once you've discovered your troublesome routines, you can improve them—no matter how small or insignificant the offending system may seem. Sometimes a small tweak is all it takes to change things for the better.

In order to de-stress your mornings, you may decide to pack lunches at night (adding this to your chore list or chore cards). Or you might choose to set your alarm ten minutes earlier and get the task you dread most off your plate. Before you know it, your mornings are humming right along and you're actually having conversations with your kids at the breakfast table—mission accomplished!

But sometimes, you have to work hard on a routine to get it just right. You may have to try one thing, and then another, and then another in order to find the rhythm that works best for you and your family. Don't give up! With some patience and effort, you can shape your day into a seamless stream of great routines.

This is how I feel during Holidays, or when expecting family.

What Routines need attention?
1. Evening – dinner, next day prep.
2. Fitness 3. Overall weekly.

When things aren't running smoothly in your home, you can feel pressured to "get organized" as fast as you possibly can—but improving your routines is supposed to *reduce* your spiritual clutter, not add to it. Try to focus on refining one routine at a time. When you feel confident that the new system is working well, then you can start working on another one.

You *can* plan to implement several new routines at once when you're approaching a big schedule-changer like the first day of summer break, the first day of school, or the first day back to school in January (when everyone's talking about New Year's resolutions anyway). Or perhaps you're gearing up for a major event like a move or the addition of a new family member. At times like these, your family can accept your various routine initiatives as one big change.

No matter how you do it, you'll have to be consistent for a few weeks. Adjustments to routine are challenging, especially for kids who like things to go a certain way—their way. Change is hard on grown-ups as well! It may take some time for the atmosphere in your house to brighten.

When it does, praise God and appreciate the blessing. Then allow those new habits to become fully ingrained in your family members' behavior before you start on something else. There's no gold star for whipping your family into shape! For Jesus Moms, motherhood is a long-distance run with Jesus cheering us on all the way.

Two Steps Forward, One Look Back

One important way to construct great routines for your family is to work on building your home. Yes, we're back to organizing stuff, but this time we're donning a more routine-specific mindset. We're going to organize your house for your routines.

As you analyze your everyday patterns, you may discover you're wasting time and energy by running around to get things. Rather than cluttering your spirit this way, you can choose to keep the things you routinely need right where you use them. Specifically, you can extend your Point of Use organizing efforts to include *adding* items that will help you complete your routines.

For example, you should purchase enough pairs of scissors to keep them everywhere you frequently use them. Store them in your home office, alongside your wrapping paper, and with your craft supplies. Hang a pair in your bedroom closet so you can effortlessly remove tags and trim loose threads. Keep a pair inside your coupon holder. You'll never go hunting for scissors again when you have them right where you routinely use them.

Similarly, try storing disinfectant wipes in your kitchen, each of your bathrooms, and your mudroom. Keep a laundry basket near your kitchen so you can easily discard dirty kitchen towels, messy bibs, and food-stained clothes. Near staircases, place baskets that will efficiently transport items that belong on different floors. With this kind of organizing, everything is *exactly* where you need it and you're making your routines as easy to complete as possible.

You can also streamline your routines with Loose Genre Organization. Go beyond grouping like things together by grouping not-so-like things together in activity "zones"—specific places in each room dedicated to the things you do there.

Consider a room that holds a wide variety of things—your garage. When you want to garden, you'll probably find your gardening gloves in the same box as your trowel. When you want to wash your car, your sponges are in the bucket with your Turtle Wax. Your tools are hanging together on a wall and your sporting equipment is all in the same general area.

In your garage, you store the things you need to complete certain tasks together because it's easier for everyone. You already know about zones! (If your garage is a mess and you have no idea what I'm talking about, try reading the above paragraph as more of a suggestion.)

You can organize your whole house by zones, according to the routines that happen in each room. Kids' bedrooms can contain zones for reading, playing, getting dressed, doing homework, and sleeping. You can create zones in your home office for paying bills, filing, and at-home work. Your family room can include zones for multiple family activities like reading, playing board games, playing video games, or watching TV.

Don't forget to think of your car as a zone—plenty of little routines happen there. Store tissues, wipes, hand sanitizer, and a trash bag within arm's reach of the driver's seat. Keep markers, paper, car games, and books on hand for little ones. Older kids will appreciate chargers, meal bars, and bottles of water. Be prepared to run errands in all weather with an extra pair of sunglasses, an umbrella or two, and a windshield scraper.

Family Central

Though you can make any household space (inside or outside!) more routine-friendly with a little organization, kitchens deserve special attention. Kitchens are the center of family life—so many routines take place there!

Kitchen space is at a premium, yet we use it to store numerous cooking-related items that we really only use once or twice a year. Even when we're organizing, we tend to put these things right back where they were. For an imminently practical kitchen, consider relocating them to out of the way storage spaces like your attic or basement. With a little intention, you can make room for all of your kitchen-related routines.

You probably already have a countertop Mission Control where you keep your planner, a family calendar, and a phone. You may want to keep stamps, envelopes, and other office supplies there as well. (Don't forget the scissors.)

If you're currently living in Babyland, embrace it—designate a cupboard or drawer for things like baby food, sippy cups, plastic dishware, and bibs. If your bigger kids do their homework in the kitchen, make sure you have pencils, paper, markers, and other grade-appropriate items in an accessible Homework Zone. You may also want to allocate an area near your kitchen table to hold a Bible, a devotional, and a prayer list for dinnertime family devotions.

And then there's what kitchens are made for—cooking! Keep pots, pans, and culinary utensils near your stove to help bring out your inner Julia Child. Store your everyday dishes, silverware, and cups between your dishwasher (for easier unloading) and your kitchen table (for easier setting).

Make the counter space that's closest to your refrigerator and pantry your Food Prep Zone. Store items like mixing bowls, measuring cups, and knives just above and below it, and try to keep that particular section of countertop as clutter free as possible. Of course, you may decide to keep a few small appliances there if you use them nearly every day. The gadgets and appliances you use less often should be stowed on higher or lower shelving in your cabinets or pantry.

You should also consider the kind of a cook you are when

you're organizing your kitchen. My friend Elise loves to bake, so she turned her kitchen island into a baking center. One of the island's cabinets is filled with baking ingredients, while the other is filled with mixing bowls, baking sheets, muffin tins and pie plates. Its drawers hold her measuring cups and spoons, rolling pin, and other baking tools.

Not being much of a cook, I determined to create a Baking Zone just like Elise's. Using the island this way freed some pantry space for other things. (And I'm sure my waistline has benefited from the chocolate chips being out of sight in a low cabinet.) Now I'm all set to bake away, because that's what I love to do!

Thinking Outside the Zone

When organizing for routines, take time to ponder what *you* love to do. Don't be afraid to arrange your belongings in an unaccustomed way, or to be completely unconventional. It's your house and you know how your unique family lives there.

My friend Staci loves cardmaking, but used to struggle to enjoy her hobby. She consistently wasted precious craft time by carrying her paper crafting supplies from her basement to her dining room table and back again. Then Staci realized she made cards much more often than she hosted dinner parties. She permanently moved her serving dishes to the basement and filled her dining room hutch with colorful paper, pens, and punches—so now she makes more cards!

Like Staci, you can find ways to store your hobby-related items where you'll actually use them. With more accessible supplies, you'll be able to enjoy your hobbies more frequently. You may be surprised by how a few relaxing, joy-filled minutes in your Hobby Zone can lift your spirit!

I recently realized I was keeping things we never, ever use in our family room—arguably the room we should enjoy the most. I looked around and saw an outdated stereo, an old video game system, and a whole cabinet full of CDs we never touch. So I relocated those items and brought things we love into the space instead.

Now a pretty bin holds our "hard floor" toys like dominoes and cars. The small CD cabinet hides workout paraphernalia like DVDs, exercise bands, and hand weights. (OK, I don't really *love* to exercise, but making it easier to do helps considerably.)

Our large cabinet now holds all of our board games, which we really do love—we're a game-playing family. I used to keep our games in a basement closet with the kids' toys, which made sense except that we never used them down there. We'd bring the games up, play them in the family room, and then take them back down. Now that I've moved them upstairs, we're playing more games than ever!

You, too, may have to challenge your perception of what

"should" be in your spaces. Your family is special. As you think through how—and where—you do the things you do, you'll discover unique ways to build your home. You can structure each room to support your routines, making everything easier and clearing your routine frustrations out of your spirit.

Chapter 6

The Way *You* Do the Things You Do

The easiest routines to tweak are the ones you and only you are performing. They're the mini-routines, the little things you do all the time. The ways you put on your makeup or unload your groceries. The way you replace your rolls of toilet paper. (Should the toilet paper unroll over or under? I say under. Travis says over. We do over. Submission at its least significant.)

Even these tiny routines may need tweaking, especially if you're completing them in inefficient, disorganized ways. We moms are often frustrated, not just with our family members' bad habits, but with our own—*Why do I always* do *that?* We ignore or fail to notice these procedural bugs as they chew away at our time, energy, and peace.

You may need to add a brand new routine, or just improve a current one, in order to squash these annoying habits. Because you're in total control of your personal routines, you can change them at will. You can reduce your spiritual clutter by streamlining the way you do all of the things you do—all of the ways you build your house.

Take the dishwasher. You unload it every day—if you're like me, sometimes twice! There are plenty of inefficient ways for a frazzled mom to empty her dishwasher.

She absently walks halfway across her kitchen, realizes one of her hands is empty, and turns back to grab something else. She's only half-listening to her husband's work story while she tries to figure out where to put everything. She gets distracted and leaves her dishwasher half-unloaded, then can't remember whether the loaded dishes are clean or dirty.

With a little intention, she can create a better, more efficient system. She can begin her process by planting her feet to one side of the dishwasher and unloading as much as she can right there, like her dishes, cups, and silverware. Next, she grabs "like" things that are stored together with both hands before she moves to a different part of her kitchen. She empties her dishwasher in the same basic order every time, making a well-organized mini-routine for herself.

You may be thinking, *Why bother? It's just emptying the*

dishwasher. What are you going to save, thirty seconds? Well, yes...thirty seconds, every day, for the rest of your life. But it's not just the time you're saving that's important.

Even the smallest routine can be tweaked to make the most of your time and *settle down your heart*. When you have a great routine in place, you don't have to think about it any more. Your body takes over so your spirit can relax and your mind can drift through thoughts, plans, and prayers. You may even have an inspired idea!

Great everyday routines also help you to be more emotionally accessible to your family. Though your hands are busy, your heart can focus on your husband and kids. Your mind is free to listen as your husband describes his workday or your kids tell you about their days at school.

In addition, a routinely calm, quiet heart is more open to the Holy Spirit. You may find yourself more fully enjoying the Lord's presence, more frequently lifting spontaneous prayers, and more clearly hearing His voice. Personal routines can create more space for Jesus in your day-to-day life.

When you create great routines, you're choosing to make the most of your time, but more importantly, you're making room in your heart for peace, for your loved ones, and for your Beloved One.

One Such Routine

For years, I fumbled with things that didn't belong in our house: purchases to return, items I'd borrowed and finished using, and things I wanted to give to others. The actual presence of these items cluttered my home. Worse, I'd forget to take them with me when I left and frequently had to turn around and come back.

These difficulties were so small and seemingly random that I didn't think to devise a system to address them until a couple of years ago. One day I failed to take a promised item to my mom and I was so frustrated with myself—*Hello, I'm supposed to be organized!* Suddenly, I realized that I was routinely forgetful about taking things with me. I needed a better system.

First, I placed a medium-sized plastic container by the door leading to our garage. All of the things that didn't belong in our house—from library books to Michael's returns to photo prints for friends—went right into that tub. It definitely cleared some clutter, but unfortunately, the box itself didn't help me remember to grab the items within.

My leaving-the-house routine was missing a step. Before each venture, I needed to pause and picture where I was going and what would happen once I arrived. As I contemplated my plans, thought flares illuminated the items I should bring. I hung a written reminder on the door until I'd established the new habit.

These reflective moments save me time while calming my spirit. When I'm feeling hurried and hassled, this routine step makes me slow down. It gives me the chance to adopt a better attitude and choose to be more patient with my husband and kids. Sometimes my minute of reflection becomes a quiet moment with Jesus—a recognition of His presence, a request for safety, a respite of thankfulness.

Leaving the house may not trip you up the way it does me; you probably have different aggravating habits. Listen for those frustrated-with-yourself thoughts and pay attention to your *why do I always do that?* moments. You can address those things with new routines, clearing out your spiritual clutter and making room for peace in the Lord.

Creating Great Habits

Changes to routine are really just new behaviors we'd like to establish. We owe it not only to ourselves but to our children, who learn life management from us, to have good, healthy habits.

Forming beneficial habits is definitely all about organizing *you*. If you read the first *Organizing You* book, then you designed systems for time management, chore management, and thought management. When you're instituting a new personal routine, you can use these systems to help you.

I've heard it takes thirty days to establish a new pattern of behavior (in fact, I've probably heard it thirty times which is why I remember it). So, use your personal organizing systems to jump-start a new routine for thirty days or longer. Write to-do items or simple reminders on your next thirty daily planner pages, or create new chore cards and lay them out every day for a month. By the end of your allotted time, you should be entrenched in your new routine.

Say you'd like to live healthier by staying hydrated. If you simply set a goal to "drink more water," you'll probably stop doing it in a couple of days. Instead, you can use your planner and chore cards to help you.

Try writing a "Drink four glasses of water" to-do item on thirty days worth of daily planner pages and check it off after your fourth glass of the day. Or make several chore cards that say "Drink a glass of water" and lay them out in your different time chunks each day for a month. In your planner's memo space, you could keep a hash mark record of finished glasses. I actually do this most days—sometimes keeping track is enough to get you *on* track!

Even if you haven't set up time management systems like these, you can purposely reinforce your new habits. Jesus Moms, it's not about a certain kind of organization, it's about intentionally supporting your new routines with tangible reminders that work for you!

To get yourself drinking water, write "Drink that fourth glass!" atop your general to-do list. Make your hash marks on a plain old Post-it note and set reminders on your phone. Try strategically placing "drink a glass of water" reminders on your computer screen, steering wheel, and daily devotional. Once you've settled into your new routine, you can forego these cues and enjoy a more settled spirit.

And don't forget to deliberately manage your thoughts when starting a new habit. Listen for your false, unhelpful feelings and devise thought-shots to inoculate yourself against them. When you think, *I don't have time to drink that*, be ready with *Oh yes, I have time for a sip*. Knock out *I'm not that thirsty* with *Being hydrated makes me feel better*. These may be the things you want to write on your Post-it notes!

You can intentionally use every tool at your disposal to create peace-giving routines—including organizing your belongings for them.

Yes, I have more "stuff organizing" ideas for you! Left-to-right, back-to-front, and top-to-bottom organizing are three great ways to set yourself up for success in your personal routines.

Some of you will think, *I love these ideas!* and start immediately. To some of you, they may sound like overorganizing—setting up systems you won't maintain for long. Give it a whirl and see what you think. After a week or two, you may find that these types of routines do help you clear out some spiritual clutter!

Left-to-Right Organizing

Not being a morning person, I generally start the day on autopilot. Thankfully, it doesn't take much brainpower to put on makeup or blow-dry hair, but sometimes I'm so drowsy I lose track of what I'm doing. Have you ever had the sneaking suspicion you forgot an important step, like applying deodorant? I've seen those commercials with the extremely attractive people subtly sniffing their armpits—if they do it, we all must do it.

We can perform our getting-ready routine efficiently, peacefully, and without skipping steps when we set up a little system for ourselves. I store my getting-ready items in order from left to right so my hands will naturally follow down the line. My makeup is loosely lined up in a drawer, with my moisturizer all the way on the left and my last-minute lip-gloss on the far right. In my bathroom cupboard, the deodorant is on the left, followed by hair products and toothpaste. This system aids my sleep-addled brain!

When you're about to start a sequential process, try positioning the things you'll need in order. Since we've been taught to read from left to right, our eyes and hands easily follow the progression. You can store your things this way, or arrange them just before you start a routine. Left-to-right organizing can help you relax into any step-by-step process.

This kind of organizing also helps with interruptions. Our daily activities are often so ingrained that a disruption can send us off track. When our rhythms are disturbed, we skip steps or add unnecessary ones.

Have you ever been halfway through a favorite recipe when you were interrupted and lost your place? You find yourself staring at your cookie dough, trying to remember if you already added the baking soda. You wonder which is worse, really flat cookies or really poofy ones? As you ponderously pop a few chocolate chips, you're wasting time and possibly a whole batch of cookies. Left-to-right organizing can help you avoid that spiritual clutter.

When I'm cooking, I order the ingredients I'll need on the left side of my cooking area. After I add an ingredient, I set it down on the right side. That way, when Spencer needs homework help, or Karly wants to share a story of her bear's adventures, or Oliver needs me to kiss a boo-boo, I can easily stop to pay attention to them and then jump right back in. Also, lining up the ingredients is much more efficient than grabbing and returning one item at a time—and I know from the start that I have all of the ingredients I need.

I fully realize this sounds very OCD and nerdy (two things my husband thinks I am anyway). But try employing some Left-to-Right Organizing to improve your daily routines. You'll complete every step, deal beautifully with interruptions, and save time and energy. Best of all, having everything right in front of you, ready to go, is so relaxing to your spirit!

Back-to-Front and Top-to-Bottom Organizing

You can keep your stored items in ready-to-go order as well. Back-to-front and top-to-bottom organizing are two related systems that can improve the routine way you store your belongings. When you put things away, place the freshest items in the back or bottom of the space, advancing the older ones to the front or top. This simple technique encourages your family members to use things in a timely manner.

Back-to-front organizing is especially effective when it comes to food storage. Grocery stores stock new food items behind older ones so the older items will sell first. At home, try placing your recent purchases in the back of your pantry and refrigerator, pushing forward the older items. You, your husband and your kids will naturally grab the front-and-center stuff that should be eaten first.

And this kind of organizing can help you save money on more than food. A first-in, first-out system curbs waste and keeps you from overbuying household goods. You may want to arrange things like toiletries, cleaning supplies, paper goods, office supplies, and batteries this way.

Similarly, back-to-front and top-to-bottom organizing can help you use your longer-term belongings in rotation. For example, your family members probably grab new towels from the top of the stack. When you place your clean towels and linens underneath the stored ones, everything is used equally. Nothing in your linen closet will become over worn, or grow musty from disuse.

The same general principle applies to clothing. When I put away our clean clothes, I place them at the bottoms of our drawers or hang them in the backs of our closets. Though my kids do search for their favorite outfits, once the best ones are dirty, whatever is on top will often do. With this system, they regularly wear all of the clothing on which we spent our hard-earned money!

When I'm choosing an outfit, I try to select one of the front-most items in my closet. Though I base my clothing choices on a variety of factors (the weather, my mood, my plans for the day), I love having a few front-and-center garments that I know I haven't worn for at least a week. I find this especially helpful on Sunday mornings, when my outfit options are limited to "nice" and my memory of what I've recently worn to church completely fails me. The Lord may not care if I show up in the same outfit every Sunday, but I don't want to wear the same outfits over and over—I want to enjoy my entire wardrobe.

With good rotation systems, you can enjoy all of your possessions, including things like board games, movies, toys, and hobby-related items. When I read to Oliver, I pull his books from the top bookshelf and replace them on the bottom shelf so I don't end up reading the same ones over and over (unless he insists—you know how that goes). If you use recipe cards, try replacing them in the back of each section, advancing dishes you haven't made in a while to the front.

Kids, husbands, and even moms tend to go for the convenient, front-and-center stuff that's easy to grab. Thankfully, it doesn't take any extra time or thought to put new things in the back or bottom of our spaces, just good personal routines. Try using front-to-back and top-to-bottom organizing as part of your daily routines, and see if they help your family members be great stewards of your blessings.

A Routinely Open Heart

The one personal routine I'd recommend for everyone (yes, everyone—this means *you*) is a prayerful daily planning session: allot just ten minutes a day to prayerfully prepare for the next twenty-four hours. I'm not talking about your daily devotional time here, but a separate time to pray yourself, and your household, ready for the day.

If you're not a morning person (I'm with you, Sister), you can actually perform this routine at night. Prayerfully shut down your house by closing the blinds, packing lunches, checking backpacks...maybe even laying out breakfast dishes or packing the car. Glance at your calendar and read over tomorrow's to-do list so you're ready for the day ahead. Then surrender your upcoming day to God, who holds the ultimate control of it all.

This nightly routine helps me to relax because I know everything's ready for a fresh tomorrow. I've started my family down an easier, calmer path to the front door, I'm prepared for what's to come, and I've dedicated the day to God. You may want to choose a nighttime Bible verse. This is mine:

> Be at rest once more, oh my soul,
> for the Lord has been good to you.
>
> *Psalm 116:7*

If you're blessed to be a morning person, you may want to set your alarm ten minutes earlier so you can similarly prepare for the upcoming day. You can prayerfully open up your house, raising the blinds so the sun will greet your family. A few quiet moments of planning time with Jesus will help you to greet them sunnily as well. You might like to meditate on this morning verse:

> Satisfy us in the morning with your unfailir
> that we may sing for joy and be glad all ou
>
> *Psalm 90:14*

No matter what hour you choose to review your upcoming events, activities, and tasks, you may begin to feel the pressure to go, go, go and do, do, do. That feeling is spiritual clutter, pure and simple. It's a lie, telling you that all of these things are solely your responsibility and exclusively in your control.

Jesus Moms, God is the one who's really in control. He sees us, He fully knows us, and He knows what's best for us. He holds the ultimate plan for our day, and only He can bless the work that lies ahead of us.

Psalm 90 is a beautiful scripture about how our lives and work can seem so small without God in them. You may want to make praying over this Psalm 90 verse a part of your daily planning routine:

> May the favor of the Lord our God rest on us,
> establish the work of our hands for us—
> yes, establish the work of our hands.
>
> *Psalm 90:17*

After you've done your best to plan and prepare, ask for the Lord's blessing upon your work. Invite Him into your day, opening your plans to Him. Acknowledge that He is Lord. Surrender your day to His will and rest in His care.

I can't think of a better way to prepare for a day, or a better personal routine to have.

Chapter 7

Family Routines

OK, I know what you're thinking: *Shannon, all of this routine stuff is great, but the real problem with my routines is my kids!* Those daily rough patches aren't your fault—it's them, right?

They don't want to wake up. They drag their feet when it's time to leave the house. They push food around their plates at mealtime or scarf something down in front of the fridge. They resist going to bed, hauling out as many excuses as possible. As much as you adore your children, they can clutter your spirit with frustration when they don't do what you want them to do.

To help you build your home with both hands, we're going to look at kid routines from a Christian perspective. Our God of Order created kids to thrive within the stability of great routines.

Unfortunately, the required consistency doesn't usually originate from them. It comes from external forces—and by that, I mean us, Jesus Moms.

We've all heard women say that their children force them to cook separate kid-friendly dinners and read at least ten books before bed (maybe we've said those things ourselves). But Jesus Moms, our kids don't "make" us do anything; God put *us* in charge of *them*. With prayerful discernment, we can choose our battles so that we all win. We can create great family routines.

If your kids resist a new routine, remember: you're The Mom and you can outlast them. When you cheerfully but firmly start a routine and stick with it, your kids will follow your lead. Once you establish the routine, everyone in your household will enjoy easily flowing from one thing to the next.[1]

In order to create that peace, make sure your routines are fantastic! The three components of successful kid routines all start with the letter C (this is one of those cheesy self-help devices I generally try to avoid, but it's true). You need to make your family routines Clear, Credible, and Consistent for your kids.

---

1 Moms of little babies, right now they pretty much own you and I get that. The only kid routine I'd recommend for you is the E-A-S-Y routine Tracy Hogg describes in *Secrets of the Baby Whisperer*. (While I don't agree with everything she whispers, the EASY routine is fabulous.) But the kid routines in this chapter are on the horizon for you, so keep reading!

Clear Routines

You've got to make your routines crystal clear to your children, or they may not understand what you want from them. When you tell them to "get ready" in the morning, what does that really mean? Get dressed? Or have their beds made, hair combed, and teeth brushed, too? Let them know exactly what's expected of them when they rise and shine.

In fact, set clear expectations for leaving the house, mealtimes, homework times, and bedtimes, too. Structure your routines in a natural, logical way so your kids can move from one thing to the next without much help from you. Kids appreciate small steps they can understand and an order they can follow.

For complicated routines with several steps, you can create "checklists" that display the routine's steps in order. If your child can't read yet, you can design a checklist with little drawings or pictures to represent the various parts of the routine.

For Karly's morning routine, I drew simple but brightly colored pictures of an outfit, a hairbrush, a toothbrush, and her bed (for making), then carefully printed the associated words beside them. My sister-in-law Kristen took photos of her preschoolers completing their daily tasks and created beautiful poster-sized checklists. And she *laminated* them. They're awesome.

At nine years old, my Spencer has a typed list of morning

tasks that includes showering, getting dressed, making his bed, brushing his teeth, and checking his backpack for his lunch and homework. The most dreaded item on this list, "Do your allergy spray," used to be a big battle every morning. When I added it to his checklist, I stopped being the bad guy who was making him do it—it was just on the list. *Tasks cease to be requests and become expectations when they're part of a routine.*

With clear routines on printed checklists, you'll also reduce the amount of frustrated reminding you do each day (which is a nice way of saying you'll nag your kids less). When you notice your child has skipped a step, all you have to say is, "Did you check your list?" Then they can refer to it independently and learn to complete their tasks on their own.

Be sure to post your colorful checklists exactly where your children carry out their routines. A morning checklist should be hung in your child's bedroom, while an after-school checklist might be better off in the kitchen.

And there are all kinds of variations on the checklist: dry erase boards, personalized magnets, doorknob hangers, and countless apps for your kids' electronic devices (which is probably the best way to get teens into the game). Creative solutions like this are the reason I love Pinterest![2] Explore your options and choose

---

2 You can find ideas like these on my "Fabulous Family" board at Pinterest. com/ShannonKay4J.

the systems that work the best for your children's ages and stages.

Once the routines become habits, your kids won't need the reminders any more! Your clear routines will enable your kids to learn independent responsibility. They'll feel proud, confident, and empowered as they move through their days, helping you to create a positive atmosphere in your home.

Credible Routines

Effective routines are also credible to your kids—they have to believe they can meet your expectations with relative ease. Don't ask your kids to do more than they know how to do or more than they have time to complete. To keep their routines from becoming tedious or overwhelming, include only the bare minimum of items on their checklists, and keep the wording simple.

A credible routine for a five-year-old is vastly different from the credible routine of a ten-year-old. As time passes, your kids will outgrow some of the steps on their checklist—actually, they might not even need a checklist for that part of the day any more. On the other hand, you may decide to add to their routines those things you've been doing for them that they can now do for themselves. In fact, your kids may be old enough to give some real input regarding how their routines are structured.

When Spencer started getting some serious homework, I

had him complete it right after school, just like I used to do. As I watched him struggling to settle down and focus, I got to thinking about how my husband—who gave Spencer half of his genes after all—operates. I realized Spencer might need a little free time before buckling down.

So I gave him the choice: did he want an hour break to rest and play after school, or did he want to get his homework done right away so he could enjoy the rest of his afternoon? He chose the hour break—and things got worse. He had a hard time relaxing because he knew the homework was waiting for him, and then he had an even harder time getting started on it.

After a week of this, I presented him with the same choice. This time he chose the homework-right-away routine and it instantly stopped being such a struggle. Yes, it's the same routine I'd originally designed, but now it's *his* routine. Suddenly, it became credible to him.

If your children are struggling through certain parts of the day, help *them* solve the problem by designing a new routine together. They can add tasks to their checklists (they know what they need to do!) or determine the order in which they complete the steps (which often doesn't matter anyway). Even little ones love feeling as though they're in control of their routines.

Encourage your older kids and teenagers to choose and implement routines on their own. Challenge them to think about how they want to feel when they're leaving for the day, walking into a class, and heading to bed. Ask questions like, "How do you want to feel when you wake up in the morning? …Well, what time do you think you should go to bed then?" The more input they have, the more credible their routines will be.

Husbands aren't immune to great routines, either! If there's a particular time of day you'd really appreciate some help from your husband, try asking him to fashion a new family routine with you. While you're at it, ask him if there's a part of your family's day that *he* dreads. He probably has great ideas about how your household could run more smoothly.

To keep your family routines credible, set aside some time at least once a year to assess and adjust them. This is a great task to add to your list of August tasks—that way, you'll update your routines just as your family embarks upon a new school year. Intentionally maintain clear, credible routines that grow with your kids!

Consistent Routines

Your routines also need to be as consistent as possible. This part is really up to you, Jesus Moms. If you can be cheerfully consistent, especially for the first few weeks, then you've got it made. Habits will form. Your only job then will be to recognize when something needs adjusted.

When Spencer and Karly were smaller, I had a great leaving-the-house routine. I'd say, "OK, kids, let's go!" and they'd stop what they were doing, use the restroom, wash their hands, and put on their shoes in five minutes flat.

Then Oliver arrived, and I was packing that last-minute item in the diaper bag, nestling him in the infant car seat, changing the surprise stinky diaper, buckling him into the car seat again, and generally taking a long time to get out the door—which frustrated me. To make matters worse, Spencer and Karly weren't hopping to it like they used to do.

One particularly crazy day I got Oliver all ready only to find four little shoes by the door. The big kids had obviously put them on and then taken them back off to go play! I was all ready to give them an exasperated talking to when Spencer said, "Mom, we were ready, *you* weren't!"

He was right. Sometimes I was ready to go when I called them, but sometimes I'd then leave them standing at the door for ten minutes waiting on me. I was being inconsistent and it wasn't fair. I determined not to call them until I was loading the car, and we were back in business.

Sometimes *we're* the ones who need to change. When we're not consistent, we give our kids the idea that our routines are optional. When we set a routine in place, we have to follow through *even if it's inconvenient for us at the time.*

We're the moms, and it's our job to plan clear and credible routines—but the real work is in staying consistent. Jesus Moms, it's so worth it. The reward for our consistency is a well-established routine that clears out our spiritual clutter and allows everyone to thrive.

Family Time Management

Time management is absolutely integral to great routines.

Here's where moms all over the organizing spectrum start to groan because they sense a family schedule coming. A schedule usually involves exact times—hear the robot voice: *we wake up at 6:45 a.m. and eat breakfast at exactly 7:30 a.m.* This much structure can make you feel "off" when you're not eating by 7:31. Schedules often feel strict and confining, adding to your stress level instead of lowering it.

On the other hand, a good routine allows for some flexibility within that structure. For a peaceful household, you want your family members to routinely complete their tasks at the same *approximate* time. To help everyone get with your program, try developing a family schedule with "target times" for each part of your daily routine.

Every August when school starts, I post our new "Upton Family Fall Schedule," complete with times to wake-up, go to bed, eat, and leave for school, preschool, work, and other activities. Travis, Spencer, and I (and even Karly, with help) refer to this schedule as we launch our new school-year routines. But I make sure to let my family members know that the times listed are just *target* times—rough ideas of when we want to be doing things.

Spencer's target shower time is 7:30 a.m., but I don't go looking for him unless it's past 7:45 and I haven't heard the water running. Breakfast is at 8:00, but no one notices if we're ten minutes early or late. Spence leaves for the school bus stop at 8:30, and even that's pretty loose—his bus doesn't come until closer to 8:40.

After a week on a new schedule, I usually need to adjust our routines and their related target times. Our routines shift and change into a better, more natural flow. By the end of September, I take down the schedule. We've all settled into our daily routines and we don't need it any more.

A temporary family "schedule" may be just the nudge your family needs to fall into a good daily rhythm. Target times can add structure while leaving a little wiggle room for slow starts and minor interruptions; in other words, when you spend a little extra time achieving a good hair day, you can spend a little less time eating breakfast.

However, if you're consistently rushing through breakfast, then you need to get a different hair cut—or start getting ready a little sooner.

Padding Routines for Extra Comfort

Nothing inflates a small frustration like the feeling that *now you're running late.* This is one piece of spiritual clutter I frequently fight. Even if we moms have great time management skills, being part of a family means that we don't really have control over our time. The good news is, we can use time cushions to help our family members stay punctual.

I rarely tell Travis and the kids what time we need to arrive at a destination. Instead, I tell them when we need to leave the house and pad it with a five-minute time cushion. This buffer makes a big difference when last minute "emergencies" slow us down on the way out. And if the fuel light is on, we can stop for gas without feeling pressed for time.

Like me, you may want to add a time cushion when you're planning to leave the house. Or if you feel like you're always eating late, try preparing dinner a few minutes earlier. If you think your kids could use more sleep, start your bedtime routine earlier. You shouldn't have to rush through *any* of your routines on a daily basis.

Even five extra minutes can give you an adequate cushion, ensuring that a minor holdup won't set off a "bad day." You'll also clear out some spiritual clutter by allowing yourself to slow down and enjoy your day-to-day routines. And on the days you don't need the extra time—when you're actually running early!—you can enjoy a few peaceful, focused moments with your kids.

It's amazing how a few extra minutes can help everyone in your family keep their equilibrium—especially you. Because, Jesus Moms, we know this: when a routine isn't working for one person, it isn't working for *anybody*. If one of your loved ones in particular isn't operating within your target times, then you may need to adjust your routine to them.

If you're the mom of a special needs child or a newborn, you're probably already structuring family routines around one person. Specific cases like that aside, you may need to consider the people in your family with special *personalities*. (And we all have special personalities, don't we?)

My sweet five-year-old Karly takes forever to eat a meal. I truly don't know how she makes it last so long. I used to spend far too much time and energy coaxing her to eat faster (come on, *just put it in your mouth and chew it, my Love*), especially at lunchtime. I worried she wasn't getting enough afternoon playtime, or that we'd be late for whatever came next. I was trying to be a good mom, but in reality I was stressing out over her marathon meals and generating a tense lunchtime atmosphere on a daily basis.

Changing our lunchtime routine was such a simple way to

accommodate Karly and settle myself down in the process. We now have a *very* early lunchtime. She gets to contemplate each individual pea and eat her yogurt one sixteenth of a teaspoon at a time, and I'm more relaxed about transitioning to the next part of our day.

If you're constantly cajoling someone to move faster, it may be the routine that needs to change, not the person. This can be such a simple, practical way to show love to that family member. Allowing extra time for these routines creates a calmer atmosphere for them—and for you. You can take your own breather during that time, maintaining a positive tone as you move on to the next thing.

And if the time just isn't there, if you simply don't have the minutes to give your slow poke, then surrender. Don't clutter your own spirit by fighting time itself, or fighting your loved one. Instead, set priorities. Decide what really needs to be done during that time and what can be moved to a different time of day or let go altogether. Seek peace and pursue it. Seek *joy*.

Don't Be Bored Now

We've tackled many common routine problems, but there's still one issue remaining: often our routines become so boring and regimented that our family members stop completing them. As fabulous Jesus Moms, we can choose to make our routines more interesting and enjoyable. About the time your loved ones get a handle on what you want them to do, I want you to kick it up a notch and add some joy!

When we have babies, we're always making routine things fun. Baby food comes in on airplanes. Bath time is all about the toys. Getting dressed is really a big game of peek-a-boo. One-year-old Oliver is living the high life now with the most fun routines ever!

But as our kids get older and begin doing things for themselves, we can lose that spirit of fun. I hear myself saying things like, "Please finish eating so you can play." (As you may have guessed, that one's for Karly.) And, "Hurry up and get clean in there—you're wasting water." (A Spencer special.) And, "I asked you to get dressed ten minutes ago—*go*." (Travis this time—just kidding...mostly.)

The more self-sufficient our kids get, the more frustrated we get when they're not doing things our way, in our timing. We lose our patience faster than our car keys. We can become rigid and legalistic about our rules and routines, causing our spirits to clutter up again. We're not having, or *being*, any fun.

In his letter to the Galatians, Paul heavily criticized the early Christians for relying on the rules and customs of Judaism to get them into Heaven. Even the ones who recognized they were saved by God's grace were still strictly adhering to all of their old ways, and forcing Gentile believers to do the same, just to be on the safe side. After some heavy admonishments, Paul changes his tone and expresses concern for the Galatian believers, asking them:

What has happened to all your joy?

Galatians 4:15a

When we become frustrated with our kids for not following our rules and routines, sometimes it *is* their fault and we need to take action. But often our legalism is an unnecessary thief of joy. Sometimes it's *us*, and we need to take a look at our spirits. How much fun are we to live with? Where is all our joy?

Jesus Moms, we are saved, we are redeemed. We're Heaven-bound, and we're living this life to glorify our Savior. When you're living for Jesus, life is filled with joy! As parents, it's our privilege to demonstrate this to our kids.

I must admit, my husband eclipses me in this area. Travis is an energetic, social guy who's widely known for making things fun. For example, he loves to take the kids to the grocery store.

Yes, you read that correctly. He finds joy at the grocery store. Travis pushes the cart and its little occupant ahead of him, then delights Oliver by pretending to be a monster chasing after it. He sends Spencer and Karly on missions: "Your mission, if you choose to accept it, is to find Lindor chocolates for your mom. GO!" He throws food items to the kids, which they catch—most of the time—and then throw into the cart. Luckily for them (but perhaps not so luckily for the other shoppers), I'm not there to be the heavy and stop any of these antics.

I prefer to spread joy in other, subtler ways. Specifically, I like to liven up our routines with a little singing. I sing made-up "Oliver" songs to get him through his boring routines like having spaghetti wiped off his face and riding in the car. Karly and I sing Disney princess songs while I'm blow-drying her hair—the villain songs are the best because you can really belt them out! Spencer pretends to disdain my singing but secretly enjoys it. He recently confirmed this by busting out his best Travolta moves as I sung "Stayin' Alive." (How he knew any of those moves is a mystery to me.)

Singing may not be your thing, but you get the idea. You can add unique, fun spins to your routines as well. Find the ways that are best suited to your personality, gifts, and sense of humor.

Maybe you'd like to start your kids' morning routine with a daily riddle to ponder while they're getting ready. Before you leave for work, you could share a secret family handshake. You could spice up your leaving-home routine by telling them The Joke of the Day as you pull out of your driveway. Just get a book of knock-knock jokes, stash it on the passenger seat, and knock yourself out (that was a Travis joke right there).

Use mealtimes to learn more about your older kids—even the surly teenagers—by asking a silly question of the day or getting a box of "Table Topics." I often liven up our dinnertime discussions with "Two Realsies and a Whopper." Each family member tells two true facts about their day and one false one, then the others attempt to guess which is the whopper. Because we're trying to fool each other, we end up hearing some of the day's most unusual events.

Naptime and bedtime tuck-ins are great moments to add personal, fun spins to your routines. When I'm leaving Karly's room at naptime, I say "goodbye" in as many languages as I can remember and she repeats each one. "Sayonara...Adios...Auf Wiedersehen...Shalom...Adieu...Au Revoir...Ciao." I always end with "ciao" because she finds it hilarious that some people say goodbye with an eating word. Her nap times are numbered and I am enjoying each sweet giggle.

None of your routines should be strict military regimes that make your life miserable. Lighten things up–enjoy being a child of God! Choose to make silly antics a part of your routines in whatever way is most natural to you. Find the things that give *you* joy and use them to bring a spirit of life and fun into your home.

Making Faith Routine, in a Good Way

Faith elements are the most essential components of Christian family routines. Nothing is more important. Our kids learn wonderful things about the Lord at church (and maybe even school), but our main job as Jesus Moms is to teach them about Him ourselves.

Our faith routines should also be clear, credible, and consistent. And just as with our other routines, we need to keep our family time with God from getting boring or compulsory. I try to shake up what we're doing every so often in order to keep our family spiritual times fresh and meaningful.

Earlier this year, we spent a few months gathering for family devotions and prayer before bedtime. Then there was the period when we read a "Bible verse of the week" at dinner and shared how it applied to our days. We always implement special family initiatives for advent and lent. Sporadically, I get out my guitar and our toy instruments so the kids and I can sing praise songs together (yes, I know how cheesy that sounds, but it makes me so happy).

Right now we have a jar of craft sticks with different prayer topics written on them, issues like world hunger, governments, missions, schools, health care, and the church. The kids take turns pulling one stick a day and we lift up prayers about the chosen topic. When the craft sticks are gone, I plan to initiate a Philippians 2:14 No Complaining Challenge—I'm sure that will challenge me![3]

You probably have your own faith-based routines like praying before meals and at bedtimes, or even a routine time for family Bible study—fantastic! You don't have to shake those things up if they're working well for you. For example, we have a permanent dry erase board in our kitchen for specific prayer requests. We've also chosen a landmark on the way to church to remind us to quietly prepare our hearts for worship each Sunday.

And, when my kids are heading to the bus stop, I give them a blessing. I make the sign of the cross on their foreheads and say, "God loves you and will be with you wherever you go," or "Jesus loves you, Sweetie, and so do I." That gives me joy, and it never gets old.

When you live your faith out loud with your children, you demonstrate a joyful Christian life. When you make faithfulness a part of your family's daily routines, you teach them that faith is a priority. And with faith initiatives in place, the message of Christ will dwell among you richly.

---

3 I'm so excited to offer you the free Guide to a Vibrant Family Faith through OrganizingJesusMoms.com—I'd love it if you'd check it out!

Let the message of Christ dwell among you richly as
you teach and admonish one another with all wisdom
through psalms, hymns, and songs from the Spirit,
singing to God with gratitude in your hearts.
And whatever you do, whether in word or deed,
do it all in the name of the Lord Jesus, giving thanks
to God the Father through him.

Colossians 3:16 and 17

This is why we're creating all of these clear, consistent, credible, joyful, faith-filled routines! We're clearing the spiritual clutter out of our homes—for ourselves, our husbands and our kids—and inviting Christ to dwell among us. We're eradicating as much stress and frustration as we can from our daily routines so we can claim His joy and peace as we raise our families.

Whatever your family routines are, do them with joy. Do them with faith. Do them all in the name of the Lord Jesus.

Chapter 8

Organizing for Your Family

Husbands and kids. They're the reasons why we do so much of what we do. The Lord fills our hearts with the desire to take the best possible care of them. They give us a distinctive sense of purpose: we want to be fantastic wives for our husbands and Jesus Moms for our kids.

They're also the reasons why we do *so much* of what we do. They're the reason we face eight loads on Laundry Day instead of just two. We anticipate their needs, then clean up after them. Sometimes we feel like we're "doing it all"—then we tend to forget the feel-good stuff about how blessed we are to have them!

Some of our spiritual clutter comes directly from our husbands and kids. On the one hand, we suspect we're not doing a good enough job for them. We worry we aren't the wives and moms they deserve. We doubt our capabilities and feel like we should be doing more.

Then the next moment we're deeply frustrated because *they* aren't doing enough for *us*. They're not helping out around the house enough, following our systems, or obeying our rules. We feel put-upon, overworked, and underappreciated.

These conflicting feelings clutter our spirits and keep us from fully enjoying our families. We need to find middle ground in the peaceful knowledge that we're doing our best, and so are they. And as Jesus Moms, we're in a unique position to help them do their best!

We don't have to fight losing battles with constant clutter or endless chores. Even as we take care of our husbands and kids, we can encourage them to take care of themselves. Every member of our households—ourselves included—can feel valued, successful, and appreciated.

In order to foster this kind of atmosphere, we need to work with our husbands and kids, not against them. We need to teach our children what they're capable of and start to require it of them. As Paul wrote to the Galatians,

> Each one should test their own actions.
> Then they can take pride in themselves alone,

without comparing themselves to someone else,
for each one should carry their own load.

Galatians 6:4-5

When we teach our kids to carry their own loads, we clear out our spiritual clutter and maybe even some of theirs! We instill in them a healthy sense of personal responsibility for their belongings and the general household. We prepare our children to leave the nest, not as dependent or entitled kids, but as capable young people. We give them the skills they need to become fabulous people of God.

And, you can lighten your own load enough to really enjoy their journey! When your family members chip in, you'll have more time to spend relaxing together and enjoying each other. Your whole family can work cooperatively to build your house into a loving, peaceful, and organized home.

Who, Me? *You* Do It.

Delegation, a mom's good friend.

Delegation will never be a mom's best friend, because, let's face it, it doesn't always work. We find things poorly done, half-done, or completely undone. Sometimes it seems easier to give up and to do it ourselves. But in order to teach our kids self-sufficiency, and to avoid stumbling over the clutter of put-upon fussiness in our own hearts, we need to assign chores to our children.

When I was growing up, my parents made it clear that my job was to be in school, learn as much as possible, and participate in extra-curricular activities. I was rarely asked to do chores like clean potties or cook dinner. I felt blessed because I knew kids who *were* expected to do those things, and more.

However, I also realized some of my friends weren't obliged to do the basic things I'd figured every kid had to do. They didn't make their own beds or put their clean laundry away. They never took their dirty dishes to the sink or loaded the dishwasher. They didn't even pick up or vacuum their own rooms. Their moms did *everything*. (Wait, maybe I did do some chores after all.)

My parents did an amazing job of making sure that my brother, sister, and I were able to grow up nice and slowly. At the same time, they required us to take care of our belongings and ourselves. And as members of the family, we were all expected to jump right in and help out whenever asked. The five of us were a team, helping each other out and treating each other with love and respect (you know, as well as siblings can).

As Jesus Moms, we put a lot of thought and prayer into finding that kind of parenting balance. We want to encourage our kids to contribute to the family while still enjoying the benefits of childhood. We endeavor to give our kids the perfect combination of discipline, structure, responsibility, and freedom. Paul addressed this by writing:

> Fathers, do not exasperate your children;
> instead, bring them up in the training
> and instruction of the Lord.
>
> *Ephesians 6:4*

Teaching our kids to manage their responsibilities is a big part of raising them to love and serve the Lord—but the *amount* of responsibility we delegate to them is going to be different in every family. The Lord has graced us with a wide margin between being too lax with our kids and exasperating them. As long as we're conscientiously choosing what we expect from our kids, we'll be right in the pocket of His blessing!

Even the best family organizing books (and I've read a lot of them) have these unrealistic lists of what chores you can assign to your kids. Eight-year-olds should be able to mow your lawn. *My baby and a machine with a big sharp blade? No.* Four-year-olds should be wiping off the countertops. *Right—my four-year-old can't even see the counters unless she's on her tippy toes.* Six-month-olds should be able to fold washrags and towels. *Surely she's joking.* (In this case I am joking—I haven't actually read that one.)

My spiritual clutter doesn't come from what my kids *could* be doing to help out around the house, anyway—it comes from what I think they *should* be doing that they're not. My spirit gets restless whenever I do things for the kids that they should be doing for themselves. Picking up their dirty clothes. Putting away their toys. Making their beds.

I find myself doing things like these far past the point of necessity. For example, I tied Spencer's shoes for him until he was well into kindergarten. When I saw one of his little classmates tying her own shoes, it was like a light shining into a cloudy part of my brain. Why hadn't I taught Spence to do that? It wasn't that I was trying to keep him "my little boy," or that I was afraid he would fail—it simply hadn't occurred to me.

Jesus Moms, we need to be purposeful about creating great chore allocations for our kids. Set aside some time to think through your household tasks and decide what you can realistically delegate. You can take some of the burden off your shoulders and help your kids to feel like valued family members.

Of course, you don't want to give them so much that they start dressing in rags and hanging out by the fireplace. It's not about what they can do to help *us* out, it's about what we can teach them to do for *themselves* and for the benefit of the whole family. You're not necessarily trying to unload your work; instead, you're intentionally blessing your kids with life-skills and independence.

Once you've crafted that great chore plan, you need to be intentional about preserving it. Kids grow and mature. Husbands and wives go through intermittent busy phases, at home and at work. Life changes, and the fulcrum shifts.

Once every six months or so, allocate time to review your chore distribution. This is a great task for your August and March task lists. As your kids hit new milestones of development and maturity, you can hand over more and more tasks. Jesus Moms, you can help them help you!

Changing Our Ways First

Back when I was still grading stacks of math papers in front of the television, I listened as a group of women on a talk show complained about their family members' quality of help. Apparently, their husbands incorrectly folded the towels and their kids misplaced food in the fridge. I listened (and graded) as the women fussed about having to refold towels, reorganize the fridge, and other similar things.

Even as a newlywed, these women offended my logical sensibilities. Soon the show's host verbalized exactly what I was thinking: they should be happy their husbands and kids were doing those things at all. And if the women kept complaining, eventually everything *would* be "perfect"—because they'd be stuck doing all the work themselves!

We can't expect our husbands and children to jump in and

help us if our expectations are too high. When our loved ones feel they just can't get it right, they stop trying. As Jesus Moms, we may need to let go of "our way" in order to discover the ways that works best for our families.

Often an organizational system seems just perfect to us, while in reality it's deeply flawed. The problem is that our husbands and kids are never, ever going to keep it up. I learned this early on when, as a young mom, I tackled our shoe problem. Travis and Spencer never seemed to know where their shoes were, and yet they were everywhere—all over the house.

Being the problem-solver that I am, I purchased some long, low shelves specifically designed to store shoes. They were white and clean and the shoes looked oh so sweet—all lined up, heels facing out, big husband shoes and pretty mom shoes and sweet toddler shoes side-by-side. I love shoes. "Shoe" was my first word. (Seriously.)

Of course, Travis and Spencer did not share my love of the fabulous shoe shelves. They totally ignored them. Though both guys were capable of placing their shoes on the shelves, they just weren't going to do it.

So the shelves only served to make the situation worse. Not only were we in the exact same shoe predicament, but I was deeply frustrated that my fellas weren't abiding by my system. Then I spotted some big, shallow baskets on deep clearance, and it was out with the beautiful but sadly ignored shelves, in with the instantly successful "shoe baskets."

Now, Spence and Karly are wonderful about tossing their shoes into the baskets as soon as they walk in the door. Sometimes they slip them half-off and try to flip them in. Even Little Oliver knows you head toward the shoe baskets when I say "It's time to get your shoes on." The shoe baskets aren't pretty, but you know what? No one ever, ever asks me, "Have you seen my shoes?" and my house is no longer littered with them.

A good system should make your life easier and clear out your spiritual clutter, not add to your frustration that your family won't fall in line. If a storage system hasn't caught on, then you need to rethink it with your husband and kids in mind. Make all of your systems as easy as possible for them.

When you adjust your system to your husband's way of doing things, he'll feel loved and seen. Other small improvements can help your little ones feel like big successes around the house. And when you store everything they need accessibly and well, they won't ask you for as much help.

For example, if your kids' toys barely fit into their containers, get some bigger containers or weed out the toys. You may need to lower things like coat hooks and laundry baskets so your kids can reach them. Store kids' plastic dishes and cups in a low kitchen drawer. I've read about moms who store their everyday dishes in low cabinets so their young children can empty the dish-washer without help. (Personally, I like my dishes too much.)

If you want your family members to help you, be sure to give them clear, easy-to-follow instructions (sound familiar?). When you reorganize something, take the time to calmly and positively explain to all of them why you've set up your organizational systems the way you have (credibility again). Your family members will feel better about abiding by your systems when they understand them.

And set them up for success. If you want your preschooler to set the table, keep a picture of a place setting in the silverware drawer just for her. If you want your grade-schooler to put clean sheets on his bed, then take the time to show him how to make those hospital corners. Teach your teens (and perhaps your hubby) how to use the appropriate appliances.

Then consistently show them some grace. Look the other way if the forks aren't on the correct side of the plate, or the bedcovers aren't smooth and perfect. Done is *better* than perfect. Mostly done is better than not done at all. Allow your family members to feel successful!

As Jesus Moms, we teach our kids how to live for Jesus, focusing on the Lord's love and grace while still enforcing His rules. The same concept applies to their work for us. If they're slacking off out of laziness, or doing a poor job just to get their work done quickly, then of course we need to do some enforcing. But if they're doing their best, then they deserve our grace and appreciation.

Richly Rewarding the Good

Every family has a different position on kids, chores, and rewards. Should we reward our kids in order to get them to help out? Wait, shouldn't they do chores as members of the family, without expecting a reward? But then how will they learn about saving and giving if we don't give them a little money?

We want to help our kids become functional members of our families (and later, society) without becoming entitled or externally motivated. At the same time we want them to feel seen, loved, and appreciated. This is another area in which Jesus Moms try to find that middle ground. As food for thought, I'll tell you where my family finds it—but ultimately you have to decide what works best for *your* kids.

At our house, each child has an age-appropriate set of chores they're expected to complete without external reward. Actually, we all do—no one pays Travis or me to cook or clean or take out the trash. Our kids need to know that they're just like us: important members of the family with jobs to do. So every Upton family member has unpaid chores that are simply our responsibilities.

We also do larger "family chores" with no expectation of a reward. Sometimes we wash cars, do yard work, spring clean, or complete a big organizing job together. I usually set aside time for a project like this on a clear weekday evening or a free Saturday, writing it on our family calendar in advance so no one is unpleasantly surprised.

Having said that, I also believe in giving kids small allowances that aren't directly linked to their chores. When we allow our kids to decide how they'd like to spend a little discretionary income, we're helping them learn about giving, saving, and budgeting. And after all, Travis and I both have a little "fun" money to spend, despite the fact that he's working outside of the home and I'm not. Each family member has a little money that's theirs, simply because they're members of the household.

I also give the kids chances to earn extra money by helping with special chores and projects. The more diligently they work, the more money they earn; just as in real life, hard work has its reward. Once a year, I lay bills on the counter to entice them to help me thoroughly clean the pantry, fridge, and freezer—a gross job that would otherwise involve a lot of complaining. In the summer, I regularly ask them to weed around our patio. I've been known to weigh the bags of weeds and pay per ounce!

I use other kinds of rewards when I'm assigning new chores, establishing new routines, or attempting to instill new habits in my kids. To get them off to a good start, I have of course proudly placed stickers on a classic chore chart. Actually, my sister Sarah is the Undisputed Master of the Sticker Chart in all its various forms (her past sticker chart titles include "I Can Keep My Room Clean," "Get Dressed, Glasses On, No Fussing," and my personal favorite, "I Will Not Play With My Poop").

Though the sticker chart is tried-and-true, there are many effective, inventive ways to keep track of our kids' efforts. I've punched holes in punch cards and moved colorful pom-poms from one jar to another. I've stamped Chore Passports[1] and have heard of other moms giving out Merit Badges. This is another arena in which Pinterest has ideas for everyone.

Of course, we all know reward systems are more fun if we're working for an overall reward at the end. (A completed sticker chart is pretty, but come on, is that it?) You can surprise your kids with a Major Award, or announce it in advance so they can look forward to it. In fact, you can ask your kids what they would like their reward to be—they may surprise you.

I love setting up rewards that involve family time experiences instead of stuff. A completed sticker chart never earns money

---

1 Check out the "Chore Passports for Kids" article on OrganizingJesusMoms.com—the kids and I had a ball with these! You'll find a free printable to help you create and use them successfully, along with a great list of household chores your kids can learn to complete.

around here, but it could get you a new family board game, a family putt-putt outing, a family room sleep-over, or a family movie night complete with popcorn. A hard-working kid can earn a king-for-the-day hat, a special time with Mom or Dad, or an ice-cream run (chocolate for Mom, please).

And at our house, once the chart is completed and the reward has been earned, *the successful child is expected to continue with his or her responsibility unrewarded.* They've learned how to do it and they've made it a habit—hooray! The reward is now their sense of accomplishment and my appreciative heart.

If things begin to slide, I start reinforcing the rules with appropriate punishments. There's no more discussion about getting rewarded for the task; it's now something the kids are expected to do as a part of our family. We're building our house together as a team.

Family Spirit

Family organization fosters the positive Family Spirit that Jesus Moms dream about. By encouraging them to contribute to the best of their abilities, you're building your home on the strengths of your family members. You promote solidarity by assigning responsibilities, arranging whole-family chores, and choosing family rewards. You can also build Family Spirit by emphasizing what truly makes you special—your family's faith in the Lord.

As Christians, our families are set apart. Our loved ones feel a sense of connectedness born of a shared faith. We have high expectations of how we treat each other. We want peace and family harmony to be the everyday atmosphere in our homes.

In fact, we want that love and happiness to radiate from our families! We want others to ask for our secret so we can tell them about our Lord. You, your husband, and your kids are a team, separate from the world but a great example in it.

Travis and I want our family to shine for Jesus like a star in the sky, so we discuss with our kids what "The Uptons" do and do not do. The Uptons do not yell at each other or speak unkindly to one another. The Uptons don't lie or conceal (unless there's a fun secret surprise like a birthday present involved). We help each other and reach out to friends. We do our best at school, work, and activities. The Uptons love God and follow His ways.

Often I can quickly correct the kids' behavior with a reminder about what it means to be an Upton. If Spencer wishes for more stuff, I cheerfully remind him that Uptons are happy with what they have. If Karly is ready to throw a tantrum over leaving a play date, I quietly remind her that Uptons are kind to their friends. The kids take pride in being important members of the Upton family. They take pride in being followers of Christ—a part of God's family.

Christian families are really just smaller sets of the whole family of God. In his New Testament letters, Paul frequently talks about the family of believers and how that family is organized. He tells us how all believers make up a body, one in which each and every part has important duties. And of course, the head of the body of believers is Christ himself:

> From him the whole body, joined and held together by
> ligaments, grows and builds itself up in love,
> as each part does its work.
>
> *Ephesians 4:16*

Just as Christ is the head of the church, He's the head of our families. Each member is a significant and necessary part of the family unit. Each person can, and should, contribute according to their gifts. Each person does their own work to build the family up in love, the love of each other and the love of the Lord.

Stop!—In the Name of Love

Of course, that Family Spirit starts with us. The love and respect we expect from our family members often originates in how we treat them. As we "organize" our families, we may need to clear a little clutter out of our own spirits to make sure they're getting the positive attention they deserve.

As loving moms, we never want our family members to feel like unwelcome interruptions to our busy lives. I confess that as a task-oriented person, I struggle with being interrupted. I'm often diligently focused on work when my husband or kids seek my attention. That's when I need to remember what—or whom—my real priorities are.

Jesus Moms, we didn't get into marriage or parenting to have spotless homes and plenty of time online—our loved ones are our *real* jobs, our holy gifts. Even if we're focused on a task or deep in thought, when they make a bid for our attention, they should win it.

Of course we don't have to drop everything when someone tugs on our arm. If I'm in the middle of something, I almost always say, "Wait, let me finish what I've started." (I'm a huge fan of this phrase.) While they wait, I finish typing the sentence or adding the ingredient or whatever else I'm doing—and then I stop.

I turn away from my task and make eye contact to let them know that they have my attention, for real. Hopefully, in that moment, my husband knows he is loved. In that moment, I want my children to know that while my world does not revolve around them, they mean the world to me.

Sometimes, I *will* just drop what I'm doing to love on them. I hug Spencer and kiss his cheek, knowing he'll laugh as he wipes off my lip prints. I grab Karly's hands and twirl her around. I scoop up Oliver and tickle his belly as his sweet giggles fill my ears.

I may forget what I was doing, and the kids may forget why they wanted my attention in the first place. But we don't care, because suddenly we're dancing in the kitchen. And I've learned just how important that is.

My Grandpa and Grandma Staley are both in their mid-nineties. I make it a priority to call them regularly because they love to talk on the phone. As they reminisce about raising their own children, Grandma tells me one thing again and again: "I might not have been the best housekeeper, but I *played* with my kids."

She made the time to play with her children in an era without parenting books or bloggers insisting it was the right thing to do. She played with her kids while partnering with her husband to run a farm. Her days were long and her chores were never-ending, yet she looks back on her time as a young mother with satisfaction and pride.

It's a good thing she tells me her mothering stories again and again, because I need to hear them. I have the kind of personality that craves completed chores and an orderly home before I can relax and play. The problem is, I've got it backwards. The chores can wait. The kids can't.

My goal is to play with my kids every day. This may seem like a ridiculous goal—I'm a mom, of course I play with my kids every day! We talk and laugh in the kitchen while I cook and clean. I take them to preschool, play dates, sports, and library story times, singing in the car on the way. We do little crafts and activities that I think are super fun *and* educational. I read to them before naps and at bedtime, and then kiss them goodnight.

But none of that is actually *playing*, is it? Playing is when I sort Spencer's Legos into color piles, handing him the pieces he needs for his new masterpiece. Playing is when I relax with Karly in her room, squeezing princess dolls into fresh outfits and then changing them again. Playing is when I stack cups for Oliver to knock down over and over.

I'm playing when I'm really focused on the child in front of me—doing what *they* want to do, making eye contact, listening intently. Real playing fills my kids' hearts with my love. They may not remember exactly what we did, but they'll remember that when they were kids, their mom *played* with them.

As Jesus Moms, we need to connect with our kids to raise them well. In order to train up our children in the way they should go, we need to be close enough to them that they can hear and follow our teaching. We need to play "This Little Piggy" with our babies. Or color with our toddlers. Or pretend to be the princes for our preschool daughters. Or shoot baskets with our grade school sons. Or listen to our teenager's music to see if we actually like it.

No matter how organized we are, life gets hectic and almost anything can seem more urgent than playtime. It's too easy to promise to play later while we fold the laundry now. If you're like me, then you'll have to be intentional about setting aside some time just for your kids.

Of all the scheduling and planning you do, dedicating a time to play is second only to dedicating time to pray. Just as I encouraged you to create a prayerful daily planning routine, I want to challenge you to use your organizational tools to help you set aside time to play. If you have to write a chore card, schedule time on your family calendar, or start a new routine in order to get yourself playing, then that's exactly what you should do. *You don't have to put up with spiritual clutter that makes you feel like you're not being the mom you want to be.*

Organizing for your family is really about organizing yourself. That's why my books and indeed my whole ministry are about organizing *you*. You're organizing your household and routines and family in order to build your home for Jesus. And you're the one who can encourage your family members to build it with you.

God brought together you, your husband, and your kids to form a team, and together, you can build a beautiful home that honors Him.

Chapter 9

Organizing for Your Husband

Attention Single Moms

If you don't currently have a hubby, then I totally understand why you may not be interested in this chapter. In fact, I give you my full blessing to go ahead and skip it, with one exception: please read it if you're thinking about obtaining a husband in the relatively near future. If you're engaged, dating, or even praying about beginning to date, keep reading.

Attention Married Moms

Please don't think I'm actually going to tell you how to make your husband be organized. If there was a way to do that, I would have figured it out by now. My husband jokes that his very existence will put me in the tabloids: *Fraud! Organizing Author Has Most Unorganized Husband Ever!* (Good thing we're not interesting enough for tabloids.) Note that this chapter is not called "Organizing Your Husband" but "Organizing *For* Your Husband," which is even better. At least it's far more realistic.

And Now, Organizing For Your Husband

Recently a friend asked me to write a letter to a Christian bride, a message she would read just moments before she walked down the aisle. Faced with a lonely blinking cursor, I pondered what I could possibly say to this wife-to-be. How was I supposed to give this woman—someone who was slightly older than me, living in another country, and whom I'd never met—life advice? Once I started typing, the answer was far easier than I'd imagined.

Organizing for your husband is all about *managing your expectations*. Often Christian brides (all brides, actually) go into marriage with a romanticized view of the future. Even the most independent among us expect a fifty-fifty workload split and someone to love and support us through thick and thin. So when the workload becomes skewed or the love and support don't happen the way we envisioned, we're disappointed, frustrated, and unhappy...in other words, we drag clutter into our own hearts.

In this chapter, you'll work to clear out your marital spiritual clutter, both with your husband[1] and on your own. Honestly, you and Jesus will do most of the work. While you can essentially force your kids to sort through their stuff and help out around the house, your husband is a completely different entity. But there is some spiritual clutter that you and your husband can clear out together.

Re-dividing to Come Up with a Better Solution

At some point around the time you got married, you and your husband decided on a division of labor. You may not have had a big talk about it. Maybe he instinctively took over some chores around the house, while others naturally fell to you.

If you were Christians when you got married, there's a pretty good chance you did what Travis and I did: filled out a "chore survey" during a church-sponsored premarital counseling experience. As total nerds who always want to have the right answers, Travis and I definitely gave the division of labor questions our

---

1 Throughout this book, I assume that your husband, while far from perfect, is a good guy who loves you and your kids. It absolutely breaks my heart, but I know this might not be the case for you. If your husband is abusive, I'm praying that you'll put down this book and seek help *right now*. You can contact the Christian ministry Focus on the Family at 1-800-A-FAMILY to talk with a counselor, or call the National Domestic Abuse Hotline at 1-800-799-SAFE.

best shot.

Unfortunately, our logic was flawed—we weren't working with all of the facts. For one thing, we were both living in apartments so we couldn't make informed decisions about homeownership responsibilities. Our answers were further skewed by our perceptions of what was "guy stuff" and what was "girl stuff."

On our workbook pages, we split the chores in a pretty traditional way. We agreed I'd be in charge of all the shopping, just as our moms were, while Travis would be in charge of lawn care, just like our dads (this was so easy to determine when we didn't have a yard). Of course, we were totally wrong.

After we moved into our first home, it became obvious that working in the great outdoors was not Travis's thing. He hated it, had difficulty finding the time after his long work hours, and suffers from allergies—two hours of yard work turn into two days of sneezing and watery eyes. So I gradually took over the outdoor chores, starting with flowerbed maintenance, then caring for the other landscaping, and eventually finding a teenage neighbor to mow our lawn. Travis still does some yard work, but it's now my responsibility.

As for the shopping, you already know Travis loves to take the kids to the grocery store—but only if he's holding a clear list of specific items. For Travis, shopping is like hunting: he searches out the prey with his eyes, subdues it with his hands, and lays it to rest in the shopping cart. He also adores the social aspects of shopping—playing with the kids, running into friends and neighbors, and chatting with cashiers.

I hate shopping for specific items. I don't believe in "bad luck," but let me tell you that if I'm looking for chocolate sauce, the store will be out of chocolate sauce. In fact, they will be out of my brand and size of everything. And if I do make it to the cash register with some stuff in my cart, the lady in front of me will need a price check on each and every item. Travis calls this the "Shop with Shan" effect.

I do much better with flexible purchases like clothing and gifts. Travis dislikes the pressure of making choices, so now we split the errands accordingly. In general, Travis shops for groceries and essential household goods, and I shop for everything else.

Recently I planned a lovely evening of sweet baby item shopping for an upcoming shower. However, when the evening arrived, the weather was perfect for trimming our shaggy shrubs. I was deliberating about which to accomplish when Travis offered to do the shopping. As I handed him the carefully highlighted registry list, he said, "I'm so glad you're the man in our relationship."

I laughed—but only because neither of us really feels that way. We've learned the line between "men's work" and "women's work" is imaginary. Instead, we try to split our chores in ways that coincide with our personal strengths. Over the years, we've forged a new division of labor agreement that looks very little like our premarital counseling one.

Like Travis and me, you and your husband may have set up your division of labor in a naive or gender-biased way that isn't working well for either of you. Or over time, chores may have drifted to one partner or the other even though you're not well suited for them. To the frustration of one or both of you, things are being done poorly or not at all. The angst you each feel over dreaded chores can cause tension in your marriage, and your whole home.

You can clear out this spiritual clutter by rebuilding your division of labor together. God created you and your husband with distinctive capabilities and interests, and then He brought you together for His glory. You can honor God with your marriage by working as a team to choose the chore allocation that works best for you.

First, as individuals, list the chores you personally tend to procrastinate or do poorly. Write down a few tasks you're willing to add to your plate, as well. Then prayerfully sit down together to renegotiate your deal. Make a pact to avoid discussing who does more, who's working harder in or outside the home, or who doesn't get their stuff done. Instead, focus on your individual strengths and abilities.

Look for tasks he heartily dislikes that you wouldn't mind

taking over, as well as chores you could let go and trust him to do. If a certain task or project is creating a lot of strife between you, ask yourself: does it really need to be done? Perhaps not. Maybe one of your kids is ready to take this chore over, or you could make room in your budget to hire someone else to do it.

Mowing makes Travis miserable and takes me away from the kids. And frankly, we both hate it, so we decided to hire it out. Though my hand shook the first few times I forked over the cash, I recognize that our teen neighbor earns every penny. I tell myself he's saving for college and try to forget that his mom told me he spends it all at Smoothie King. In reality, I know that the money we spend on this outside help is money invested in our marriage.

Invest in your marriage by trading chores, delegating them to your children, hiring outside help, and deciding to let go of some chores or projects altogether. When you and your husband take the time to create a great division of labor, you'll have more time, energy, and love for each other.

Allowing Him To Be Awesome

Collaborative efforts, like jointly developing an effective division of labor, are pretty much the extent to which we can "organize" our husbands. After that, it's up to us, Jesus Moms, to purposefully build our homes with our husbands in mind. Just as with your children, you have the unique ability to make your husband feel valued, successful, and appreciated around the house.

That great division of labor will make him feel valued at home, as will showing him you desire his opinion on other household organizing projects. As I mentioned previously, you should ask for your husband's input on your family routines and systems. And when you're organizing a space in your home—especially one that's more "his" space—offer to include him in the process. He may have some great ideas to share, and the two of you may come up with better systems cooperatively.

In order to help him feel successful, you need to choose a level of structure he can maintain—even if that means molding your routines and storage systems around him. And when you cheerfully explain new systems and routines to your kids, make sure your hubby is front and center. He'll be much more likely to get excited about (or at least tolerate) your organizing efforts if he comprehends the reasoning behind them.

The most important way you can help your husband succeed at household endeavors is to *not* do something: don't go around criticizing or redoing what your husband does. Unless there's an actual safety issue, Jesus Moms, let it be not quite how you would have it. After all, there's no eleventh commandment declaring that your way is the right way to do things. His way will almost certainly do. When he hears enough critiques or sees you "fixing" his work, it will soon be your work.

In fact, I want you to go in the opposite direction and praise him for a job well done—or at least *done*. You can verbally thank him, write him little notes, kiss him on the cheek, give him little gifts, or even plan a special night out. (You may be picking up traces of Gary Chapman's *The Five Love Languages* here—best marriage book ever, besides the Bible!) When you show your husband your appreciation for the work he does, in the home and out of it, you're loving him in a special, intentional way.

If you're feeling hard-pressed for appreciative feelings, try to see your husband's efforts as Jesus sees them. See your husband as a beloved child of God. Allow that while he's imperfect, he's doing his best for his family and his Lord. Recognize that, just as you do things he doesn't seem to notice, he takes care of things that fly under your radar. Pray for a thankful heart and let your hubby see the work God's doing in *you*.

Some Work He's Done in Me

People often ask me in a very jolly tone, "So, is your husband organized like you?" I can't help but laugh a little. "Heh, heh, heh...no."

Now I hope you're not reading that as an evil villain laugh, because it's not that kind of laugh. It's more like a slightly ironic

"I'm amused by your question" laugh. Travis is definitely not organized in the way I am. But when people ask about it, I'm quick to tell them that Travis is so brilliant at his job he doesn't *need* to be as organized as I am. This is mostly true; it's definitely true enough to be able to say it and really mean it.

Travis *is* organized. He's one of those people who keeps many piles of stuff and typically knows what's in them. He uses an online calendar for work. After years of messing around with different electronic daily planner systems, he's back to good old paper. Heh, heh, heh. (OK, that one was mightily close to the evil villain laugh.)

Travis recently read me this quote: "Ladies, if a man says he will fix it, he will. There is no need to remind him every six months about it." He was laughing—but he was serious. He doesn't want me to organize him. He's happy how he is.

Travis is hit-or-miss with many of my systems, including the could-not-be-simpler shoe baskets. He views walking around and looking for his shoes, and all of his other stuff, as a part of life. I know I can't force him to be any neater and I've stopped trying. As the years have passed, I've learned to ignore Travis's piles of stuff in more and more areas of our home.

I've decided not to be bothered by the clutter on or in his dresser, his nightstand, his side of the closet, the basement, or the garage. I've learned to deal with the stuff he leaves around the more communal parts of the house without feeling frustrated, as well: every morning after he leaves for work I gather it up and gently place it in a pile in our home office, a room I've completely disowned. He doesn't love that I do that, but he knows it's just how I am.

I don't love that he leaves his things wherever he happens to stop using them, but I know it's just how he is. It took me some time to realize that, after all, *these are not his systems*. Travis truly doesn't care where he puts his shoes, or anything else. Mess doesn't bother him. He's simply being exactly how God created him to be.

Now, I'm not claiming to be perfectly patient and accepting. Sometimes there's a rebellious part of me that thinks, *Come on! I don't let the kids do this. Get with the program, Buddy. Pick up after yourself. Put your shoes in the darn basket. I am not your momma or your maid.*

No, I'm not his mom and I'm not his maid. If I were his mom, I'd be able to *make* him pick up after himself, and if I were his maid, at least I'd get paid. The wife in me wants to feel hurt because he knows how much it bothers me and he does it anyway… but the Jesus Mom in me knows better. The fact that he leaves his stuff all over the house doesn't mean he loves me any less than he should.

If your husband doesn't do things your way, it might be because it's just how he is, how God created him to be. The fact that he doesn't do things the way you'd like him to doesn't make him an inherently bad husband, *nor does it mean he loves you any less than he should.* These issues are simply ways for you to show your love for him through submission.

Submission

For the rest of this chapter, I'll be challenging you to change your attitude rather than try to organize your husband. (Please read it anyway.)

Submission is a necessary part of running any household with a husband in it, yet the word "submission" is controversial, even in Christian circles. Let's set aside any negative connotations we may have about that word and consider *real Biblical submission*. The loving, respectful kind of submission described in places like Ephesians 5 and Colossians 3. Consider this verse, as well:

> Do nothing out of selfish ambition or vain conceit.
> Rather, in humility value others above yourselves,
> not looking to your own interests but each of you
> to the interests of the others.
>
> *Philippians 2:3-4*

This is relatively easy to do for our kids—it's practically a biological imperative! But it's much harder to do this for our husbands, especially when *we're* running the household: setting up routines, delegating chores, and organizing the stuff. Home life feels like our responsibility, so it's hard to accept that our husbands have the final say over it.

When you and your husband are facing off over an issue, and a Biblical case can't definitively be made for one side or the other, then it's an Ephesians 5 situation. If possible, Christian husbands and wives are to bend to one another in the mutual submission that's called compromise (Ephesians 5:21).

But sometimes, you'll want something from your hubby that he won't give, or he'll ask something of you that you don't want to surrender. Rather than have us live in perpetual tension, God gives us clear instructions for resolving conflicts within marriage. Your husband is supposed to choose sacrificial love for you (Ephesians 5:25-33). You're supposed to choose respectful submission to him (Ephesians 5:22-24).

You can't force your husband to agree with you or abide by your decisions. You can't even make him do his part—sacrificial love must be freely given, not demanded. *You can only do your part.* You can, and should, submit.

Travis and I work together as a parenting and house-running team as much as possible. When we disagree, I'll stick to my guns if it's a matter I feel very, *very* strongly about (usually something concerning the kids). But in all other cases, I've learned to submit—usually after an unnecessarily long internal struggle.

I feel more relaxed in a neat, clean home; Travis functions just fine with marginal mess. I like to be on time; Travis doesn't see anything wrong with being a little late. I need to complete my chores before I can relax; Travis can just as easily wait until tomorrow, or the next day, or the week after that; there is no need to remind him every six months about it. We are vastly different people.

I spent the early part of our marriage trying to get Travis to come over to "my side"—my ways seem so logical, so reasonable, so right! I regularly became uptight and upset when things didn't go my way. Then suddenly, when Karly was born and I found myself struggling with postpartum anxiety, I was forced to examine how I cope with life. Mess, being late, and things not being done triggered off-the-charts anxiety and panic attacks for me...yet Travis was still Travis.

Some spiritual clutter can't be organized—you have to surrender it to the Lord. Perhaps He allowed me to suffer with clinical anxiety for so long because He wants me to fully understand that *I am not in control*. The Lord is in control. It finally dawned on me that when it comes to mess or time or to-dos or anything else, I cannot change Travis. I realized that I'm the only one in this marriage I can change, so I began to submit.

I've made the prayerful choice to surrender many things. There are chaotic parts of our home, but I can overlook them. We're a few minutes late for church almost every Sunday, but I choose not to worry about it (The Good Lord knows *I* would have been there on time!). I've learned to recognize that most things really can wait until tomorrow, or next weekend, or six months from now. Living with and loving Travis has made me into a more relaxed person.

No matter how much you organize, you can't make your husband keep up with your storage systems or follow your routines or do the chores you want him to do. If you harbor resentment about these things, *you* will clutter up your own spirit. You'll live in continual conflict, resisting God's perfect design for your marriage. You'll miss the peace and joy that come from submission.

To Nag or Not To Nag

No wife wants to be a nag, and it doesn't work anyway. The more we ask for something to be done, the more odious the job seems to the person we're asking. If you're repeatedly prodding your husband to complete a certain task, ask yourself these questions:

1. Can I do this myself? If so, try to do it with a happy heart.

2. Does this really *need* to be done? If not, try to surrender it

with a happy heart.

3.   Can I hire someone else to do it? If so, try to pay them with a happy heart.

4.   What can I do to help and support my husband in this task? If he's the only one who can complete a necessary task, help him. Allocate time for him to work on it (and take the kids out of the house if that would help), purchase the necessary materials, and support him in any way you can.

I almost never get to the end of this little progression—I usually call myself out with the first question! Just as I did in our original division of labor agreement, I frequently ask Travis to do things based on gender bias or my dislike for a task, not because the task suits his strengths.

After nagging Travis to take out the trash (a task he doesn't mind but I truly despise), I submitted and started doing it myself with as happy a heart as I could muster. I literally prayed my way through taking out the trash: *Lord, thank you that I'm capable of taking out this trash. I thank you that we're blessed enough to have this much trash. Please help me not to be resentful.*

And wouldn't you know it, shortly after I stopped nagging him and took over the chore, Travis started taking out the trash! I guess we split the job pretty evenly now, but I'm not counting. I still despise it, yet the Lord has blessed me with a peace about it, a peace I was missing by asking Travis to do it over and over again and growing ever more irritated by his lack of response.

Ending the nagging cycle isn't always that easy (not that the whole trash thing felt particularly easy at the time). Sometimes you really have to lay something at the Lord's feet. A couple of years ago, the Lord called me to submit to Travis about family dinners. Even after I'd relaxed many of my other marital expectations, I was holding on to this one for dear life.

When I was a kid, my family had dinner together every night. My dad arrived home from work at the same time each day and we sat down to a family meal. We talked about our days, my little brother made fun of the way I ate, and my little sister made sure I didn't get more food than her. Typical family stuff (at least I thought it was typical).

Then I got my driver's license and an after-school job, and the dinners became more sporadic. When I went off to college, I missed our dinners more than any other part of family life. And so, as a new mom, I instituted family dinners as soon as Spencer could sit up in a high chair. I wanted to cherish our time as a young family, and in my heart of hearts I believed that family dinners are integral to a happy childhood.

I spent *years* trying to get Travis to family dinners. At first I asked him to call me if he was running late, but he'd call to say he was leaving work fifteen minutes after I had dinner on the table.

Then I tried setting a later dinnertime, ignoring the rumbling tummies and increasingly fussy moods of the kids, but Travis stayed at work later still. I tried to convince him to go to work a little earlier so he could come home earlier (who wants to spend all that time in rush hour traffic, anyway?). It didn't pan out.

Travis and I shared many, many frustrated words over this topic and ruined many an evening. He thought I didn't understand his workload or schedule. I didn't understand why he wasn't making our family a priority. On a nearly nightly basis I worried he was involved in an accident because he hadn't called, and then I was mad when he *did* get home because he'd missed it, again.

What I really wanted was for Travis to set a consistent family dinnertime and then call me if he was running late. This didn't seem like much to ask, but it finally dawned on me that it was too much pressure for him. It just wasn't going to work that way. *Ever.*

With prayer, I surrendered my desire for family dinnertime. It was really, really hard; I cried over it with Jesus. Then I told Travis that the kids and I were going to eat at 5:30 p.m. each day. If he wasn't home, we'd just eat without him, no big deal.

Now I enjoy my meals with the kids and ask them about their days whether Travis is home or not. He's fine jumping into dinnertime at the end or eating after we're done. He doesn't even seem to mind the lukewarm food (and my cooking isn't great when it's hot). The kids are just happy they get to eat when they're hungry.

In fact, it's obvious that the only one who really cared about family dinnertime was me. I was the one delaying the kids' dinners, causing the marital tension, and filling my own spirit with clutter. By insisting on my own way, I was missing out on peaceful, joyful dinners with my kids. The Lord showed me that submitting is infinitely better than attempting to badger my husband into doing what I want.

Jesus Moms, you can't nag your husband into doing things your way, and you shouldn't even try. Instead of focusing on what your husband isn't doing, pray about what *you* can change. Discover the huge capacity the Lord has given you to go above and beyond for your husband. With prayer, you can be the giver in any household-related situation, and the Lord will fill you up again.

If You're the Travis

You may be reading this chapter from Travis's standpoint—perhaps *you're* the one who isn't as neat or doesn't enjoy a structured routine, while your husband wishes you'd run a more orderly household. Though I'm lacking in empathy, I have plenty of sympathy. The household is your domain, and I imagine your husband telling you how to run it gets old pretty quickly.

The good news is, when your husband craves more structure

than you do, you can really organize for him! Everything in this chapter still applies: Renegotiate your chore allocation. Collaborate on organizing systems wherever you can. Then, in the same spirit of submission, try things his way.

Start with specific issues that bother him and determine to change them. It's almost certainly not your *whole* house driving him crazy, no matter what he says. We all have particular things that bother us more than others. Give him the gift of peace by alleviating those tensions for him.

If he's frustrated by a lack of clean underwear, make a goal to do more frequent white loads or buy some more boxer briefs. If he hates being late, resolve to be ready five (or ten, or fifteen) minutes earlier than you normally would. If he'd really appreciate a neater home, try doing a quick household pick-up in the mornings, before he gets home from work, or just after the kids go to bed.

If he wants you to do something in a certain way or store things just so, why not give it a try? What a meaningful, demonstrative way to show your husband you love him! Ask the Holy Spirit to bless you with energy for your tasks, as I did (and sometimes still do) when taking out the trash. And look for the good reasons your husband has for wanting things handled his way.

On the other hand, if there's a good reason you'd like to do things *your* way, let him know. We Type-A's usually appreciate logic. Set aside a time for the two of you to prayerfully discuss your family routines and storage systems, just as you did with your division of labor talk. Be sure to lower your defenses so you can really hear what he says.

Marriage isn't a what-he-wants versus what-you-want proposition anyway. It doesn't matter who likes more structure or who's read more organizing books. Your goal is to foster a cooperative mentality and support your husband as the two of you raise your kids and run your household. As smart, capable people united in love, you can build your home together much more successfully than you could individually.

No matter how "organized" your husband is, I'm writing the same thing to you that I wrote to that Christian bride: organizing for your husband is all about managing your marital expectations. Not about lowering them to a "realistic" level, but about aligning them with *God's* expectations.

God expects great things from your marriage, Jesus Mom, and He expects great things from you. Team up with your husband to create a great division of labor. Adjust the way you do things to help him feel valued, successful, and appreciated. In humility, honor your husband above yourself and submit to him.

Choose to clear out the spiritual clutter you're harboring about your husband—make room for God's blessings of peace and joy in your marriage.

Chapter 10

Walking in Faithfulness Through Your House

Jesus Moms, we're going to pull it all together now.

You've read about sorting and organizing your stuff. You've pondered your personal and family routines. You've contemplated how to organize for your kids and your husband. You've been building a bigger bucket, studying The Word, and giving thought to your ways.

Now, we're going to consider the final, unseen member of our households: Jesus. He's going to make our work complete. We'll invite Him to pervade our thoughts and plans as we build our houses for our families. Quite frankly, we can't do it without Him.

What truly sets Jesus Moms apart, what makes us special

among women, is our dedication to Jesus Christ. If there's one thing we know about building a house, it's this:

Unless the Lord builds the house,
those who build it labor in vain.

Psalm 127:1a

All of our careful thought and work would mean nothing if we were doing it apart from Christ. So let's take a moment to make sure we're inviting Him into the homes we're so carefully building.

Making Room for Jesus on Your Path

When I was a freshman in college, I lived in a dorm on the outskirts of campus. At first I enjoyed the hike to the main buildings, down a long path and across a picturesque bridge. Then, just as my commute was becoming tiresome—and chilly!—my religion professor unexpectedly presented me with an antidote to the tedium.

On that day, he instructed my classmates and me to close our eyes while he read aloud from the Bible—we were to do nothing but picture ourselves at the feeding of the five thousand. We were there, sitting on that hot hillside, surrounded by real people, hearing the clear and strong voice of Jesus talking to the crowd.

Our professor encouraged us to feel the dust between our toes, the cloaks on our bodies, and the hunger in our bellies. We imagined what it would *really* be like to witness Jesus miraculously turning a few loaves and fish into enough to satisfy thousands of people. I was filled with a new sense of wonder.

After class, I enjoyed trying this technique with other passages of scripture. I also began to visualize Jesus in a clearer, more present way when I prayed. On my commute to class, I found myself walking in the middle of the path, leaving space at my right hand for Jesus to walk beside me.

At first, it felt a little dumb—I also had to be careful that I wasn't running into people or getting hit by bikers—but I also felt His loving presence with me in such a real way. Next, I began clearing off the passenger seat in my car when I drove home for a visit, so I could better imagine Jesus traveling with me. When I prayed on my knees, I envisioned Him standing next to me with His hand on my head.

Over the years, I've continued to meditate on God's presence this way. Jesus sat on my hospital bed through each of my three labors. After Karly was born, I fought my deep anxiety—particularly the worry that something bad was going to happen to Travis or the kids—by curling up on my bed and picturing us all being held gently in God's cupped hands.[1]

Now I visualize Jesus sitting with me while I fold laundry or clean, and it helps me to focus on my conversation with Him. I ask Him to bless and keep any person on my heart. When I feel anxious or down, I turn my worries over to Him. When I'm faced with a tough situation, I ask for ideas about what to do and try out words to say.

When I picture Jesus with me, He's warm, relaxed, and loving, even if He's telling me I need to straighten up my act. (And, rather than the traditional robe, He's always wearing well-worn jeans and a red plaid flannel shirt, with a short, well-trimmed beard and bare feet—the mind is an interesting thing, isn't it?) In my heart I'm like Moses, sitting in his tent and talking with the Lord face to face, as a man speaks with his friend.

Knowing Jesus is always with me, and picturing Him alongside me as I complete my household tasks, brings me a deep sense of peace. He will never leave me nor forsake me. He calms my heart with His promise:

> And surely I am with you always,
> to the very end of the age.
> *Matthew 28:20b*

---

1 For more about how the Lord helped me with my anxiety, check out the "Reducing Anxiety with Jesus" article on OrganizingJesusMoms.com. If there's one article I want you to read, it's that one!

Jesus Moms, the Lord is with you throughout your day, even the most boring, wearisome parts. His Holy Spirit lives inside you and wants to bless you with a spirit of peace. As you walk through your house, make room for Jesus on *your* path.

Try picturing Him beside you—smiling at you, comforting you, radiating His love. Ask Him to keep you company as you do laundry, clean, or exercise. Let your heart rest in Jesus and your mind wander over the thoughts you can give to Him. What a perfect way to invite Him into your home!

You and Jesus in Each Room

You can invite the Lord into your home in more tangible ways as well, purposefully adding elements that remind you of His presence. My friend Debbie lights a certain scented candle when she wants to be close to the Lord, particularly during her devotional time. Her "Jesus scent" relaxes her body and helps her mind focus on Him. She told me that though she enjoys working hard to *be* Jesus to people, her scented candle helps her to treasure being *with* Him.

All moms struggle with that type of spiritual clutter from time to time, the tendency to lean more toward our inner Martha than our inner Mary. We take care of so many people and do so many things that our hearts become distracted from the reason we're doing it all in the first place: the love of our Savior! As we build our houses, we can use reminders like Debbie's candle to keep Him at the forefront of our thoughts.

I have another friend named Sarah who loves to buy framed inspirational quotes for her home. And she's not limited by what's available for purchase—when she finds a faith-filled quote that speaks to her, she prints it out and frames it herself. She hears Jesus speaking directly to her through these words, and by decorating her home with them she's choosing to listen every day.

I invite Him into my home by filling it with Christian music. I truly enjoy most kinds of music, but while secular songs can momentarily lift my spirits, they don't fill my heart with joy and peace like my Jesus Music does. Praise and worship music helps bring His presence to glorious life for me!

The sights, smells, and sounds of your home can all remind you to connect with Jesus. You may be creative enough to find spiritual reminders in textures and tastes as well (the Lord knows that I love wrapping up in a soft blanket, and I often thank Him for chocolate). Consider your surroundings—at home and at work— and try something new to remind you of His presence. Invite Jesus to dwell with you richly.[2]

---

2 For ideas about how to invite Christ into your home at Christmastime in particular, check out the "More Jesus at Christmas!" article on OrganizingJesusMoms.com.

In fact, God may use the faith-filled elements in your home to impact more hearts than just yours. Our houses aren't just dwelling places, they're tools He uses to influence people for the Kingdom of Heaven. Likewise, Christian hosting isn't simply a social art; it's a ministry, a calling.

As we build our homes, we can dedicate them to glorifying the Lord. Through our hospitality, we can encourage and inspire other believers. We can also form a foundation of friendship with nonbelievers, one that may prepare their hearts for our Christian witness.

When Spencer's new friend "Joe" visited our home for a play date, he naturally took a good look around Spencer's room. "You've got a lot of Jesus stuff in here," he observed. "Do you go to church *every* week?" Spencer confirmed this and asked Joe about his own church background, which was sparse. Then Spencer described a typical Sunday morning at our church, and Joe agreed to come with him to check it out.

This conversation almost certainly wouldn't have happened without the cross on Spencer's dresser, or the Christian poem hanging on his wall, or the Bible and other faith-centered books in his room. If these things can get nine year old boys talking about faith, then you never know what may happen with *your* friends![3]

---

3 For fun get-together ideas, check out the "Party Hearty!" article on OrganizingJesusMoms.com. Yes, I'm referring you there again…I just couldn't fit everything I wanted to share into the book!

When your guests feel the peace and love in your home, make sure they can easily deduce the reason for them. Let the wall hangings in your living room, the devotional on your end table, and the Bible on your kitchen counter clue them into the fact that Jesus is a member of your family. And if they comment on any of those things, you'll have the perfect opening to share with them about your less tangible (and sometimes harder to bring up) faith.

I intentionally hung scripture-filled plaques on our front stoop and above each entryway so no visitor to our home can miss them. A recent caller said, "Wow, that's very Jewish." I took that as a huge compliment!

> These commandments that I give you today are to be
> on your hearts. Impress them on your children.
> Talk about them when you sit at home and when you
> walk along the road, when you lie down and when
> you get up. Tie them as symbols on your hands and
> bind them on your foreheads. Write them on the
> doorframes of your houses and on your gates.
>
> *Deuteronomy 6:6-9*

Jesus Moms, fill your home with visible scripture—write favorite verses on the doorframes of your house and on your gates! Your guests will notice them, your kids will read them, and your husband will know how important they are to you. You may not notice them *every* day, but they'll be there when your heart needs them.

Every room in your home can demonstrate your faith in a unique way. You can display scriptures about healthy bodies in your kitchen and healthy relationships in your family room. Fill your bedroom with verses about marriage and rest, and your kids' bedrooms with scriptures that make them feel loved and protected. Appendix C will help you get started— It's a list of appropriate verses for each room, which I call "Roominations." Soon your whole house will be filled with God's Word, and His presence.

The House Walk

So once you've invited Jesus into your home, how do you actually organize it for Him? Where do you begin?

> By wisdom a house is built, and through
> understanding it is established; through knowledge its
> rooms are filled with rare and beautiful treasures.
>
> *Proverbs 24:3-4*

As Jesus Moms, we want to seek understanding about how our homes are running, and wisdom about how to organize them. And we want to fill our homes with the love, knowledge, praise, and presence of God, like rare and beautiful treasures!

166

As soon as you can, I'd love for you to do what I call a House Walk. We've been building up to this, Jesus Moms! You're going to walk through your home with Jesus—talking with Him about it, filling up with knowledge about how it's functioning, and making an action plan to organize it with love.

For a good House Walk, you'll need to have your home to yourself for a few hours of quiet concentration and prayer.[4] It's best to walk through your entire house in one session, but if you can't find someone to watch your kids for that long then you could pray through one floor at a time or even one room at a time.

As you enter each room, pray for God's presence to fill that room, now and always. Thank Him for the people and things that reside there on a daily basis. Ask for His blessing upon your family and over all of the activities you complete within those walls. Finally, ask Him for clarity and wisdom as you view the room with His eyes.

Then take a good look around. What's in here that shouldn't be? What belongings are difficult to access? What does your family do in this room, and is it set up to support those routines? How can you help your family members to enjoy this space? *What clutters your spirit about this room?*

Appendix B contains a step-by-step description of this pro-

---

4 Or you can invite your husband to join you on your House Walk. Both of you may cherish the time you'll spend praying and planning together!

cess and includes a comprehensive list of questions to guide you as you walk. Take a notebook and pen with you so you can catch the spiritual clutter bubbling up to the surface and pop it into writing. As you take your House Walk, you'll want to jot down all of the things that come to mind: to-dos, things to buy, projects, and long-term plans.

Don't give in to the temptation to start "doing" during the House Walk. Even one or two "quick things" can distract you and cause you to waste time and energy. Even if a task would only take a few moments, write it down. You'll enjoy getting that easy checkmark on your list later. Right now, you're simply gathering knowledge.

There's another reason not to jump in and start organizing until after you've completed your House Walk: you'll have new ideas and make new connections as you move through your home. You'll recognize that this particular item needs to move into that room—and this over here could take its place. Then you'll realize you don't need to buy a certain item because you can actually use the thing from over there...and this container can hold the stuff in that room.

You'll find things to organize together in groups, items to place strategically for your routines, and ways to accommodate how your husband and kids truly function—all at the same time. Your brain will be firing on all cylinders and you'll be planning for the big picture! Once you've walked and prayed through your whole house, organize your notes by creating separate lists for quick to-dos, projects, things to purchase, and long-term plans.

Plan to perform a House Walk once a year to keep up with your growing and changing family—this would be a great thing to write on a January or July task list. Even the most organized moms can have a hard time keeping up with the changes life brings to a home. Things sneak up on us!

As I prepared to write this book, I took a House Walk. Despite my "organized" status, I surprised myself with *long* lists of things to do, buy, and consider. A light in our basement had been out for ages—it drove me crazy but I always forgot about it when I went back upstairs. My bathmat was completely falling apart, but I was so used to it I didn't realize what bad shape it was in. Travis's Christmas present from me was just sitting in our closet, but after some thought I knew just where to place it so he'd actually use it.

All of these things were causing me spiritual clutter. Things like the light bulb, the bathmat, the unused present...they niggled at my heart. Yet they were simple items to add to my to-do lists and shopping lists. Though most of the changes were small, together they felt like a vast home-improvement and added a great deal of peace to my spirit.

My recent House Walk also prompted me to make the bigger, routine-related changes to our family room that I described at the end of Chapter 5. Reorganizing my family room was a size-able project, but a joyful one! Because of my House Walk, I'm enjoying my home and family more than ever before.

Your lists will be filled with similar items, big and small... and you'll have to choose not to be overwhelmed by them. You've prayed over your whole home, and now you're fully aware of the changes you want to make.

Yes, you have lots to do, but Christ is still on the throne. Don't be afraid of the work—use it to glorify God! You've taken a huge step by gathering the knowledge and covering your home with prayer; now, you can start to build it piece by piece.

Finding the Time...or Making It

After you take your House Walk and you know exactly what you want to do, it's time to make a plan and get to work. You do have to be intentional—if you wait for the perfect organizing op-portunity to fall into your lap, it may be a while. You don't want your House Walk lists to sit around untouched, filling your heart with even more spiritual clutter.

Now's the time to follow through as the Proverbs 14 Woman we studied in Chapter 1. You've decided to build your house (vs 1), so work like an ox and line your manger with good things (vs 4).

You've given thought to your ways (vs 8), now choose to live in uprightness so your family can flourish (vs 11). You're planning what is good to find love and faithfulness (vs 22), so work hard to bring profit (vs 23). With the Lord, build a secure fortress, a refuge for your children (vs 26). It's time to clear out the clutter and bring in the peace, because a heart at peace gives life (vs 30).

If you've read *Organizing You*, the time management skills you learned will help you to build your house efficiently and well. Each day for the next week or so, choose a few things from your House Walk "quick to-do" list to write in your planner. If you discovered tasks you'd like to perform on a regular basis, create the associated daily, weekly, and monthly chore cards and make notes on your monthly lists. Add the items on your House Walk shopping list to your Errand Day lists. And of course, your Project Day is the perfect time to tackle your larger House Walk projects.

If you didn't read the first book, then you can simply make a master to-do list and start working on it, one checkmark at a time. Or your husband may be willing to take the kids out on a Saturday so you can organize away (thank him profusely, even if he has an ulterior motive). Look at your family calendar and set aside a time to get started—then schedule the next time, and the next.

When you're planning for larger projects, be sure to break them down into manageable pieces and plan for *the first step*. Staring down an entire room, a big storage space, or any sizable project can be completely overwhelming; it's tough to get started and difficult to keep going. If you're feeling less than confident about your ability to do the work, you'll soon need a chocolate break, which could deteriorate into a nap.

There's another problem with trying to complete a large project in one fell swoop: it almost always takes longer than you think it should. It's sad but true: organizing projects look worse before they look better. You don't want to weigh down your heart with the "worse" view at the end of your organizing time, no matter how well spent it was.

Instead, choose a realistic portion of your project and make that your goal. Focus on one thing at a time so you can get it done and feel great about it! When you meet that mini-goal, give yourself a happy checkmark on your to-do list—then schedule a time to complete the next step in your project. It takes time to build a house!

Every Jesus Mom will handle her House Walk lists differently. Some of you will be able to focus during large chunks of time and will subtly transform your home in a week or less. Some of you will parcel out your projects over a month or two, feeling encouraged by the small but steady changes. The important thing is to keep going, to create a sense of momentum. Let the joy and pride you feel about the changes you're making give you energy for the tasks ahead.

Little by little, you'll organize your entire home and store all of your belongings in a neat, accessible way. You'll prepare for your routines and your days will flow smoothly. You'll make it easier for your husbands and kids to come alongside you as you manage your household. You'll be walking through your house in faithfulness, and with a thankful heart.

The Doorstop Mentality

Until you've tried it, you may wonder if giving such deliberate thought to your house won't give you *more* spiritual clutter. Won't you think of things you want but don't have? Or ways you wish your home was, but isn't? On the contrary, a good House Walk with Jesus puts all of your blessings in evidence, giving you a renewed sense of purpose and peace.

Of course, much of the spiritual clutter related to your home is actionable. During your House Walk, you'll see things that really need to be done, like belongings to be organized and new ways to accommodate your husband and your kids. But you've got to guard your heart against the negative thoughts you *don't* want to organize—clutter you can only clear out by giving it to your Father.

While the thought *I'd be happier if I had a bigger closet* may have a smidgen of truth to it, it's not helpful and it's certainly not biblically grounded! Similarly, if you find yourself thinking, *I can't relax until this project is done*, think again. We're called to be content in all circumstances.

And if you look around and think, *I can't have anyone over until I get this place straightened up*, the physical mess isn't the problem. Instead, your spiritual clutter is keeping you from God's will for your home. God doesn't tell us to wait until everything's perfect to host His children, He calls us to practice hospitality without grumbling.

While you're walking through your home, be sure to examine the knowledge you're gaining in the light of God's truth. Is what you're thinking true, necessary, and helpful? If so, then get busy organizing. But if not, choose to seek peace and pursue it. Ponder what the Lord would say about the issue and fight your spiritual clutter with the truth that you are deeply blessed.

My husband and I call this having a "Doorstop Mentality." We coined the phrase in honor of my Grandma Kelley and her amazingly upbeat outlook on life. She seems to see only the blessings surrounding her. My dad once said that if we gave her a box of rocks for Christmas, she'd proclaim with sincere gratitude that she'd been in desperate need of a doorstop!

When Travis and I refer to the "Doorstop Mentality," we're talking about more than positivity or optimism. The glass isn't just half-full, it's half-full of the exact beverage for which you were thirsty. A person with a Doorstop Mentality stops negative thoughts in their tracks and keeps the door wide open for joy.

Jesus Moms, when you take your House Walk, practice your Doorstop Mentality. Let gratitude push any looming clutter out of your spirit. Choose to dwell on God's lavish grace—because of it, you have precious children to cherish and a home full of love in which to raise them.

In fact, try to keep a Doorstop Mentality as you walk through your house every day—and let your kids hear it! When you hear good news, praise Jesus out loud. When a little one gets a boo-boo, verbally thank the Father for keeping her from greater harm. At the end of a rough day, place your hand on your child's head and say, "Thank you, Lord, for my sweetheart." Use your very breath to blow the clutter out of your spirit.

Recently I was helping Karly put away her Hungry Hippos game with its twenty marbles. I counted the marbles as I picked them up—seventeen, eighteen, nineteen...no twenty. Immediately I started searching for the lost marble, worried it would find its way into little Oliver's mouth.

A few seconds later I found it, and said with a sigh of relief, "Thank you, Jesus."

Karly said, "But Mom, Jesus didn't find that, *you* did." Oh, how wrong she was! Our kids need to know—to be told and shown—that *every* good thing comes from the Lord!

Let your kids see and hear you give God the glory for every good thing in your life. Tell them about the Doorstop Mentality. As you survey your home, show them that your heart is filled, not with spiritual clutter over what you do or don't have, but with appreciation for His blessings.

Your Abundant Life in Christ

On the first day of third grade, Spencer came home with a grin on his face and something special in his backpack. He reached in and pulled out (drumroll please)...a planner! He was almost as excited as I was—after all, it's very "grown up" to be expected to maintain a planner. Throughout the year, Spencer used it to keep track of his assignments, spelling lists, and special reminders. He didn't forget a Crazy Hair Day all year, and that delighted my heart.

I do want my kids to learn how to keep themselves organized and I try to get them involved in my organizational systems. Spencer and Karly know exactly where my planner is and place items that need attention directly on top of it. They know our family routines and how to check our family calendar to see what's coming up. They generally know where to put away their belongings, and where to find them. They even know to add their favorite foods to the grocery list (although that doesn't guarantee a purchase).

But even better, all three of my kids can show you the exact spot where I like to read my Bible. They see me doing my devotions. They hear me pray out loud when I'm scared, worried, or thankful. They listen as I tell them stories about how the Lord has blessed our family over the years. They know that ultimately I am not in control over our home or over them—God is.

No matter what level of structure you choose for your household, you can set an example of intentional, abundant living for Jesus Christ. You don't have to be "organized" to live *all in* for Jesus, you just need to find the level of organization that enables you to be effective for Him and for your family.

Organization is a powerful tool to wield as you pursue true abundant living. Jesus Moms, be intentional. Organize enough to keep your home functioning smoothly. Use organization to clear the clutter out of your spirit and your home as you see fit. And allow the Lord to lead you.

> He tends his flock like a shepherd:
> He gathers the lambs in his arms
> and carries them close to his heart;
> he gently leads those that have young.
>
> *Isaiah 40:11*

The Lord loves your children and holds them close to His heart. He entrusted them to your care, and gently leads you as you love and parent them. Through His Word and the Holy Spirit, He will give you all you need to raise your kids in a faith-filled household. He will help you to build your home with strength and beauty.

In Exodus 26, God describes exactly how He wanted His own house, the tabernacle, to be built. He orders the many frames and crossbars to be made out of strong acacia wood. But then He asks for them to be painted with gold and hung with velvet. His house had a core of strength, covered in beauty.

Jesus Moms, your home's core of strength is the Lord, our Almighty God. Your home's beauty comes from the work of your hands, the love in your heart, and the beautiful spirit He's created within you. Walk through your home in peace and faithfulness, claiming your abundant life in your loving God.

Afterword

Jesus Mom, you made it to the end! I hope you feel edified, encouraged, and challenged. I hope you've discovered ways in which Christ is calling you to be more like Him. However, I don't want you to leave this book with the sense that you "should" be doing what I'm doing—or what anyone else is doing—in order to be a great mom.

You already are one.

I'm deeply impressed by your open spirit, your desire to learn and grow, your bravery.

I'm proud of you for diligently striving to serve the Lord and your family, for being *all in.*

And I've been praying for you. As you've read this book,

you've been covered in prayer.

Just as I love to give my kids blessings, I'd like to leave you
with one:

May you find joy in your home and your family, my sister.
May the Father bless your household and the work of your hands.
May the Spirit's peace fill you and guard your heart against anxiety.
May you grow closer to Jesus each day and live in His abundance.

Much love to you,
Shannon

And the peace of God, which transcends all understanding, will guard your hearts and your minds in
Christ Jesus.

Philippians 4:7

About the Author

Shannon Upton

Shannon Upton is a Christian
speaker, writer, and mom living in
Central Ohio. Her books, talks, blog,
and website are all devoted to helping
her sisters in Christ clear the clutter
out of their schedules, homes, and
spirits.

You can stay in touch with Shannon in several ways. For
continued Jesus Mom encouragement, check out:

OrganizingJesusMoms.com

Facebook.com/Organizing*You*Ministries

Pinterest.com/ShannonKay4J

Twitter.com/ ShannonKay4J

If you have any further questions, or if you'd like Shannon to
speak at your church or women's event, please feel free to e-mail
her directly at shannon@organizingjesusmoms.com.

Study Guide

Getting a Bigger Bucket

These questions will help you apply the concepts in *Building Your House* to your home! They're meant for individual study, or for discussion points if you're reading this book with a friend. If you'd like to study this book with a group of friends, be sure to check out the *Building Your House* Six-Session Group Bible Study, free through OrganizingJesusMoms.com!

Study Guide
Chapter 1

- Do you tend to worry about how you're doing as a wife and mom? How do you think God feels about the job you're doing?

- What are the top three things you're anxious about? How do they hold up in the light of God's truth? Do you need to surrender them, or are there some actions you need to take in order to live *all in* for Jesus?

- What does a "Jesus Mom" look like to you? How do you envision her home?

- Do you tend to pursue perfection or pursue peace? What would "organized enough" look like to you?

- Are you ready to dive in and get to work, or is a part of you holding back? What do you need to do to open your heart to this process?

- Most importantly, what is Jesus speaking into your heart through this chapter?

Study Guide
Chapter 2

- Are you, your husband, and kids frustrated by your family's level of clutter?

- Do you have a false sense of urgency about making changes? What's a realistic timeline for your organizational efforts?

- Are you waiting to feel peaceful until after you've organized? What's an area that you need to surrender right now, before you begin clearing out the clutter?

- Is there a deeper, emotional issue that has you gripping your stuff too tightly? If so, where can you seek Godly counsel?

- Are some of the things you need and love inaccessible? Are your storage spaces (like closets, cabinets, shelves, and drawers) overflowing? Can you picture a realistically neat version of these spaces?

- Take a few minutes to try the Hundred-Years View and the Near Future View on your belongings. Actually walk around your home and picture your family in the different rooms. Jot down some of your feelings and ideas. You may even want to draw a picture of your (realistic!) plans.

- Is your house filled to capacity, and then some? Ideally, how full would you like your home to be—85%? 80%? (Do I hear 75%? Sold!)

- And again, most importantly, what is Jesus speaking into your heart through this chapter?

Study Guide
Chapter 3

- What would make your organizing time more fun—playing music, asking a friend to help sort, or working for a personal reward? Or would those things distract you?

- What are your counterproductive organizing habits and hang-ups? Do you try to tackle overwhelmingly large projects, or get mired down in decision-making? How would you like to prepare your heart for the time you'll spend organizing?

- When you tackle a sorting project, do you tend to be more of a keeper or a tosser? What are the drawbacks to being the way you are, and what are the benefits?

- Do you have a hard time letting go of sentimental belongings? How can you preserve your memories without keeping the actual objects?

- What things in your home do you see as one big group—an informal collection? Do you need and love all of the individual items in these collections?

- Do you have any special or sentimental collections? Are they still really special to you? If so, how can you downsize, display, or actually use these items so you'll really enjoy them?

• Are there some things that, for whatever reason, you absolutely have to keep even though you'd let them go if you could? What spiritual clutter are you harboring about those things—resentment, frustration? How can you surrender those emotions to the Lord?

• And again (you may be sensing a theme here), what is Jesus speaking into your heart through this chapter?

Study Guide
Chapter 4

- How functional are your current organizational systems? Is your natural tendency to be overorganized, underorganized, or somewhere in the middle?

- Do you wish for the organized spaces you see in magazines or on Pinterest? How can you surrender these perfectionistic ideals to God and look at your home with contentment?

- Right now, is there an organized space in your home that you truly love? What makes it work for you?

- In general, what's the least amount of structure that will make your things the most accessible? What's "organized enough" for you?

- Are there things spread out in different parts of your home that could be kept together in groups?

- Are your things at their point of use? What should be stored in each room, and what shouldn't?

- Do you need to cut back on your spending to reduce the flow of stuff into your home? How do you want to approach your nonessential purchases? (If this is a deep-seated issue, where can you seek Godly counsel?)

- What's your favorite way to get used items to people who could use them—yard sales, online selling, or straight donations? Which is the easiest for you and gives you the least spiritual clutter?

- Is the stuff in your home taking away from your focus on your family and on the Lord? How can you foster an attitude of contentment in your home?

- Most importantly, what is Jesus speaking into your heart through this chapter?

Study Guide
Chapter 5

- Do you resist the idea of creating intentional routines? What's holding you back?

- What trips you up day after day? How can you change your routines for the better?

- What kind of tone do you set for your family in the morning? When you're leaving the house? Or coming home? Around dinnertime? Bedtime? What about other stressful times of day?

- Is there anything you routinely have to do that clutters your spirit? How can you surrender your antipathy and dedicate this work to the Lord?

- What "duplicate" items can you place strategically around your home in order to make your routines easier?

- What zones can you set up in the different rooms of your house in order to better accommodate your routines? In particular, is your kitchen set up for daily success—even ease?

- Are there any unconventional ways you can place your belongings exactly where you use them?

- Most importantly, what is Jesus speaking into your heart through this chapter?

Study Guide
Chapter 6

- Do you get frustrated with yourself for doing the same ineffective things over and over again? As you think through a typical day, what things stand out?

- What mini-routines do you complete each day? How can you be more efficient within these routines?

- Is there an unavoidable routine that you dread? How can you surrender that spiritual clutter to the Lord and relax into the routine?

- What are some new personal routines or habits you'd like to start? How can you get them rolling?

- How might you use left-to-right organizing to streamline your routines and take the sting out of interruptions?

- How might you use front-to-back and top-to-bottom organizing to help rotate the use of your things and save money on perishables?

- Are you willing to dedicate ten minutes a day to prayerful planning, at night or in the morning? What Bible verse would you like to meditate upon as you prepare for your day?

- How would your "normal" day be different if you surrendered each and every part of it to God? If Jesus took your place for a month, how might He do things differently? What would Jesus change about your routines so you could better love yourself, your family, and Him?

- Most importantly, what is Jesus speaking into your heart through this chapter?

Study Guide
Chapter 7

- Do your family routines give your home a feeling of stability? What do you want the atmosphere of your home to be like?

- Do your kids know exactly what's expected from them as they move through the day? How can you make your routines more clear?

- Are your routines too simple or too complicated for your kids? How can you make your routines more credible?

- Do you have older kids or teens who may want to devise their own routines? What about your husband?

- Are you as consistent as you need to be with your family's routines? What's one area you can focus on this week?

- How do you feel about creating a family schedule with target times? Would this restrict you, or ease your spirit?

- How often do you find yourself running late? Which of your daily routines need a little more time to complete?

- If a member of your family is really struggling with a routine,

STSTUDY GUIDES

how can you adapt the routine to them?

- If it's simply not possible to complete a routine the way you'd like, how can you surrender your frustration and adjust your expectations?

- How can you make your routines more fun for your family? What kind of special touches can you add that really suit your personality?

- Do you incorporate your faith into your family's daily life? How can you use family routines to teach your kids how central, how crucial a relationship with God really is?

- Most importantly, what is Jesus speaking into your heart through this chapter?

196

Study Guide

Chapter 8

- Are you doing things for your kids that they could do for themselves, or are you expecting too much from them? Where's your ideal balance?

- What are some age-appropriate chores you can realistically delegate to your kids?

- What are some systems that work for you but don't work for your husband and kids? How can you change your ways in order to accommodate how they're more likely to do things?

- Do you give clear instructions and guidelines when you ask for help around the house? Are your husband and kids able to feel successful at home?

- Are you holding onto a piece of spiritual clutter about your family that you just can't change, no matter how organized you are? What does scripture say about it? How can you surrender it to your Father?

- How do you feel about reward systems like allowances, chore charts, and special treats? If you used a reward to encourage your kids to start a new chore system or routine, when would the rewarding stop?

- Do you have a strong family identity and bond? What family chores and family rewards would encourage more family time and unity in your home?

- How do you handle your husband and kids when they interrupt you? Do you let them "finish what they've started" when you interrupt them? How often do they get your undivided attention?

- How can you find the right balance between work and play? Is that an area of mothering you feel led to improve? If so, how can you use your organizational systems to help you get started?

- Most importantly, what is Jesus speaking into your heart through this chapter?

Chapter 9

- Do you expect too much out of your husband in the areas of household help or family life? How can you clear that clutter out of your spirit?

- How is your division of labor? Is he feeling put-upon, or are you? Are there any chores that you and your husband could rearrange according to your strengths?

- When your husband does household work, do you try to help him "do it right," criticize his efforts, or redo what he does? How can you relax and enjoy the help he's giving you?

- How do you feel about true, Biblical submission?

- What are some expectations you need to let go of in order to honor your husband? Write specific prayers to help you surrender those things.

- Do you tend to nag your husband about household chores or tasks? Can you take on some of those things yourself, let them go, or hire them out? If not, how can you support his efforts to complete them?

- If your husband is more particular than you, can you try his way of doing things?

- What are two or three things that drive you bananas about your husband? Are they just facets of who God created him to be? Can you surrender your spiritual clutter about those things and choose to accommodate him with a generous heart?

- Most importantly, what is Jesus speaking into your heart through this chapter?

Chapter 10

- Would you like to use visualization techniques while reading scripture or praying? What does Jesus look like to you?

- Think of times when your body is busy but your spirit is free to converse with Jesus. How can you make room for Him on your path?

- How can you place more tangible reminders of the Lord around your home? Are there scripture verses you'd like to frame? What about songs or scents you can use to grow closer to God?

- Would an unchurched visitor in your home be able to tell that Jesus is a member of your family? Do you have "conversation pieces" that can help bring up the topic of faith?

- When will you complete your House Walk? And what's your plan to accomplish the tasks you'll discover?

- Do you frequently dream about additional belongings or home improvements? How can you quiet those thoughts and foster a Doorstop Mentality instead?

- Are you a positive example for your kids when it comes to living an intentional, abundant life in Christ? How can you become "organized enough" to be an effective woman of God?

- Do you feel the Lord gently leading you as you parent your kids? As you've read this book, how have you grown closer to your family and to the Lord?

- Most importantly, what is Jesus speaking into your heart through this chapter? Can you summarize how He's been leading your heart through this book?

Appendix A

A Step-by-Step Guide for Sorting Through Any Space

ORGANIZING
you

1. Choose a small space. (Divide larger spaces into smaller, manageable sections.)

2. Pray over the space. Pray for wisdom, energy, and contentment with your portion. (You may want to read Mark 10:17-27, Luke 12:13-21, and Psalm 16:5-6.)

3. Clear out the space completely and clean it. Be sure to add to the pile any other belongings you'd like to store in that space.

4. Do a Quick Sort into five piles: Keep, Elsewhere, Maybe, Give, and Toss/Recycle.

5. Sort the Maybe Pile into the other four piles, using these questions:

- When was the last time I used this?
- Is it out of date?
- Does it work well for my family?
- If I were standing in a store right now, would I buy this again?
- If I'm not using this, can I bless others with it?

- If I unexpectedly needed it, could I borrow or buy another one?
- If it has sentimental value, is there a way I can preserve the memory without keeping the item itself?
- Do I *need* it?
- Do I *love* it?

6. Take out the trash and recycling.

7. Donate the Give Away items, list them online, or price them for your next garage sale and put them into storage. (Be sure to write any related to-do items in your daily planner.)

8. Put the Elsewhere items away, deciding exactly where they go and creating spaces for them if necessary.

9. Assess the Keep Pile items (if any). Determine how you'll store them neatly and accessibly, using these questions:

- How and where do I use these items on a routine basis?
- How do my family members access these items? What kind of system will help them to help me?
- What's the *least* amount of structure that will keep my belongings the *most* accessible?
- How organized is "organized enough" to clear out my spiritual clutter?

Appendix B
A Step-by-Step Guide to
The House Walk

ORGANIZING
you

1. Kick off your House Walk by inviting Jesus to join you. (I'd recommend prayerfully listening to "Invade" by Watermark, or at least reading its fabulous lyrics.)

2. In each room, begin by lifting up thanksgiving and requests as you feel led. You may want to anoint the doorframes with oil or pray for protection from the enemy. (For specific things to pray over in each room, check out Appendix C.) Ask God to open your eyes and grant wisdom to your heart.

3. Survey the room as a whole. Then start at the entryway and work your way around the perimeter. Look in the middle of the room, at the ceiling, and at the floor. Look in the cabinets and drawers. Really *see* everything in the room.

4. Write down all of the spiritual clutter you have about that particular room. Here are some things to consider:

- Think about your actual stuff. Is everything stored so you and your family members can access it easily? What can you group together? Are there any overgrown collections you need to cut back? What doesn't belong in here at all?

- Think about your family's routines. What do you do in this room? Are there any stumbling blocks to those routines? What items can you bring into this room to make life easier?

- Think like a homebuilder. Does anything need cleaned? What really needs replaced? Is everything safe? Are there any repetitive "upkeep" tasks to write on chore cards or your monthly task lists?

- See it as a visitor. If you were a stranger walking into this room, what would you see? Do you actually like the room arrangement, wall hangings, and knickknacks? Do things bother you that you just don't see any more?

- See it with the eyes of Jesus. Is there anything in this room contrary to His presence (like inappropriate books, movies, or video games, or things causing strife between members of your family)? How will the people who visit this room know it belongs to the Lord?

- See it with His grace. What's just a temporary situation that can be overlooked for the time being? What's cluttering your spirit about this room that you need to surrender to the Lord? What circumstances are calling for intentional contentment?

5. As you move from room to room, note the ideas you have and connections you make. Find the best possible use for your things. Use the storage solutions you already have to their fullest.

6. Complete the walk through your entire house. Don't forget rooms like the laundry/utility room, bathrooms, garage, basement, and attic. Walk around the outside of your home as well, considering the house itself, your yard, and your car.

7. Take the notes you've made and change them into actionable items. Make separate lists of:

- Quick to-dos—write them in your planner.
- Projects—determine the first step toward completing each of them, then write those first steps as to-dos in your planner.
- Things to Buy—add these to your shopping lists.
- Long-Term Plans—keep this list in the back of your planner with your Goal List.

8. Block out work time on your family calendar. (You may want to review the "Finding the time...or making it" section in Chapter 10.) Then build your home with love!

Appendix C
Roominations

ORGANIZING *you*

This is a list of scriptures you may want to pray over during your House Walk or even display in each room. Of course, there are so many more—this is just to get you started! May Jesus fill your home with His sweet presence.

Family room

Pray over: joyful relationships

Scriptures: II Corinthians 5:7, Psalm 118:24

Dining room

Pray over: your hospitality

Scriptures: Matthew 18:20, Proverbs 17:17, I John 3:1

Kitchen

Pray over: healthy bodies and lifestyles

Scriptures: Psalm 34:8, I Corinthians 10:31, John 6:35

Your bedroom

Pray over: your marriage

Scriptures: I John 4:19, Proverbs 5:18,

Colossians 3:18-19

And pray over: your rest

Scriptures: Psalm 32:7, Psalm 4:8, Psalm 116:7,

Psalm 23:1-3

Kids' bedrooms

Pray over: your individual children

Scriptures: Psalm 139:14, Jeremiah 29:11, Jeremiah 5:1

Bathrooms

Pray over: positive self-image

Scriptures: I Samuel 16:7b, I Peter 3:3-4,

Ephesians 6:14-17, Proverbs 31

Laundry room

Pray over: a clean heart

Scriptures: Psalm 51:10, Isaiah 1:18

Study/office/craft room

Pray over: your work

Colossians 3:23, Micah 6:8, Proverbs 3:5

Playroom

Pray over: your kids' relationships with each other

Scriptures: Psalm 127:3, Proverbs 22:6,

Zephaniah 3:7, Matthew 19:14

Basement/attic

Pray over: your stored goods and memories

Scriptures: Matthew 6:19-20, Psalm 111:4,

Proverbs 10:7a

Entryways and doorways

Pray for: protection over your home, comings, and goings

Scriptures: Joshua 1:9, Proverbs 3:3, Proverbs 24:3-4,

Joshua 24:15, Isaiah 43:2a

Appendix D
Scripture List

ORGANIZING
you

Chapter 1: Proverbs 13:1, 4, 8, 11a, 22, 23, 26, and 30a, Psalm 34:14

Chapter 2: Mark 10:21-22, Timothy 6:6-7

Chapter 3: Ecclesiastes 3:6

Chapter 4: Psalm 16:5-6

Chapter 5: I Corinthians 14:40

Chapter 6: Psalm 116:7, Psalm 90:14, Psalm 90:17

Chapter 7: Galatians 4:15a, Colossians 3:16 and 17

Chapter 8: Galatians 6:4-5, Ephesians 6:4, Ephesians 4:16

Chapter 9: Philippians 2:3-4

Chapter 10: Psalm 127:1a, Matthew 28:20b, Deuteronomy 6:6-9, Proverbs 24:3-4, Isaiah 40:11

Another Great Book!

Organizing You

Shannon Upton's unique blend of organizational techniques, relatable personal stories, and scripture got its start in her first book, *Organizing You*. In this book, Shannon helps Christian women to organize

their time, chores, and thoughts with Jesus. Shannon also offers a Free Six-Week *Organizing You* Group Bible Study. Find out more at OrganizingJesusMoms.com!

"*Organizing You* is fun, refreshing, and full of practical ideas for making life easier so you can savor each minute with your family and live life with Jesus. You'll finish this book feeling good about yourself and eager to put your new organizing ideas into place!"

-Christy, stay-at-home mom of four

"If you're feeling overwhelmed and weighed down by the chaos in your life, look no further. Shannon's sense of humor and helpful tips leave you feeling empowered and equipped to make some easy changes that will help you live peacefully in the presence of Jesus."

-Sarah, working mom of three

"*Organizing You* isn't your typical organizing book! Shannon brings to light that by clearing out any spiritual clutter you may be harboring, you can walk with Jesus throughout your days and live with more intention for Him, your family, and you!"

-Jaime, homeschooling mom of four

Find more information about *Organizing You* at

www.OrganizingJesusMoms.com

The book is available for purchase from all major retailers including Amazon.com and BarnesandNoble.com. Ask for it by name at your neighborhood bookstore.